YOUNG LOVE

IN SIXTIES

BRISTOL

Chris Walker

First published 2017

Revised and updated 2019

Copyright @ 2017 Chris Walker

All Rights Reserved

The names of some individuals in
Young Love in Sixties Bristol
have been changed

ISBN-13: 978-1546575399
ISBN-10: 1546575391

Typeset in Garamond 13

CONTENTS

1. What's it all about?   1
2. Early Days   5
3. The First Love   9
4. Beyond the First Love   12
5. Moving On   18
6. Youth Clubs   26
7. Down Town   31
8. The Swinging Sixties   41
9. Scooter World   47
10. Banking Opportunities   55
11. Karen   61
12. Another Surprise   70
13. Marilyn   74

continued…

14.	Variety is the Spice of Life	83
15.	Not always about Girls	93
16.	- but it usually was	106
17.	1966 and all that	113
18.	Lily - Part 1	120
19.	Lily - Part 2	126
20.	Jackie	138
21.	If Music be the Food of Love	146
22.	Getting There	150
23.	End of an Era	154

1

WHAT'S IT ALL ABOUT?

Young love - yes indeed, there was a fair amount of that in the 1960s, but also a fair amount of young lust.

This is my life during the 1960s, a true story being told as it happened. It is not a work of fiction but a personal account of how it was for me, pure and simple. Well, not always pure. When I left school at the end of 1961 as an innocent teenager, I had no idea of the emotional encounters I was to discover over the subsequent years.

As a result of having a job with a bank and joining a couple of clubs in Bristol, I was fortunate to have opportunities throughout the 1960s to enjoy the company of many delightful girls. But I was no Casanova. The majority of these friendships were short lived, although some did bless me with moments of innocent pleasure. And on rare moments, not so innocent pleasure. Only a select few of my adventures were to become serious. More on all that later.

A word about my job - these days, one might not wish to advertise having worked for a bank, but in the 1960s banking was an honourable profession. It is no longer the case, of course, and I was glad to get out when I did. I might mention also that branch banking, where I worked, has always been a world away from the discredited investment banking.

The occasional diaries I maintained throughout the decade have provided a skeleton on which to build my story, but these records were not always required as I remember certain events so very clearly. These I will cover in some detail and occasionally graphic detail. When pulling my thoughts together, I found it difficult at times to describe some of my experiences without resorting to clichés. Sorry about that. There is a saying, 'Avoid clichés like the plague'. On the other hand, I heard an argument recently claiming that clichés develop for a reason.

In an attempt to create a relaxed flow of dialogue, I have taken a few liberties with the niceties of grammar. When I recall an event vividly, I might slip into the present tense but I am, of course, writing about the past. Some activities have been amalgamated for a better understanding, and a few names have been changed to defend the modesty of the girls I was privileged to meet. Otherwise this is it, a progression from a naïve innocent to a sexually educated adult. By necessity some sexual references have been included. My reflections might rekindle in others, memories of *their* teenage romances.

I do not shy away from describing some of my more intimate and personal exploits; my thoughts and memories are an open book. I must emphasise my activities *then* do not represent the way I might behave today, given similar circumstances. Chance would be a fine thing.

Regrets? I've had a few, and a few of those I'll mention. I regret not always behaving with honour and whilst I cannot change the past, I apologise sincerely to those I may have hurt through my, at times, inexcusable behaviour.

Conversely, I regret not taking advantage of several opportunities presented to me, as often I was slow on the uptake. This resulted in me being a late developer on the sexual experiences front. There were too many instances when a young lady would make what I took to be just an idle comment, or an action such as a hand on my shoulder, or perhaps on another part of my body. Only later would I realise, 'She was asking for a date' or even, 'That was an invitation to go further'.

On his deathbed Sir John Betjeman, the former Poet Laureate, when asked if he had any regrets, replied,

'I wish I'd had more sex.'

I have some sympathy with that. But there were times when I did seize the moment.

2

EARLY DAYS

I met my first love in 1962. Did she know she was my first? Does she recall that first moist kiss? Did she realise I was so inexperienced? Very soon I will record my time with Janet, but first a short digression to summarise the lead up to me moving to Bristol and later meeting her. Please stay with me, I will, in the following chapters, describe a variety of exploits in Bristol, some leading to embarrassments, confessions and humiliations - but also some successes.

My first brief encounter with a girl, if it could be called that, was in the summer of 1961 when I endured a holiday job at a chicken processing factory, Walden's of Trowbridge, near where I lived in Wiltshire. My allocated duties included picking feathers missed by the chicken plucking machine (I don't know if it was actually called that). During tea breaks, cup of tea one old penny, I would attempt to sit next to Carol Williams, a pretty girl I knew from primary school. When I was successful in so positioning myself, I would cringe with self-consciousness should she pass a fleeting glance in my direction. I never spoke to her: what if she had actually spoken to me? I would be frozen to the spot. Not literally, of course. My success with girls could only get better.

My second memory of any form of girl interaction, or inaction, was also in 1961. Hayley was one of three daughters of a family who were close friends of my parents. She and I knew each other, albeit not very well, from family camping holidays when we were very young. Hayley attended a secondary girls' school in Trowbridge and I was a pupil at the adjoining boys' school. One day, across the hedge separating the two schools, our eyes met and we gazed at each other for a brief moment or two. That was it, nothing more. But it was then I realised we were no longer very young. We were to meet up later on a very agreeable and intimate basis.

Another encounter across the same school hedge involved David, a school pal blessed with a most impressive mop of champagne white hair. He was relatively short like me, although it was David who stood out in a crowd. He vaguely knew an attractive girl by the name of Pam Shadwell who was a pupil at the girls' school. When she was spotted, he would call across the hedge, but fairly quietly so there was no danger of actually being heard,

'Does Pam Shadwell shag well?'

Sex was on our mind as we had just received a sex education lesson from Doctor Matthews to learn about such matters, the aim being to fill in the gaps in our knowledge. We were young and immature and I don't think we learnt much from the session, we thought we knew it all. We considered ourselves quite adventurous, daring even, evidenced by David's school hedge comment. In reality we knew very little.

I later saw Pam in a grimy second-hand record shop down a back street in Trowbridge. There was no way I would have the courage to speak to her, and certainly not to ask for a reply to David's question. She was returning a record, 'Goodness, Gracious Me', by Peter Sellers and Sophia Loren, (second hand, of course), because she didn't like the track on the 'B' side. She got her 2/- (10p) refund. After she left the shop the proprietor turned to me and spoke with a heavy sigh,

'Some people.'

I returned to my perusal of the record racks, attempting to expand my meagre collection of singles. I was inwardly kicking myself for not at least saying 'Hello' to the girl.

It was now the end of December 1961. I left school and moved to Bristol with my family as my father had been transferred to a new job in that fine city. I was just 16 years of age. Towards the end of my school days I was becoming aware of girls and thought they might be nice, but didn't understand them.

On arrival in Bristol, my education in this respect was to begin.

3

THE FIRST LOVE

'The first love is an emotion which is tender, violent, painful, beautiful and impatient, an amalgam of the deepest feelings in a new discovery. We remember our first love when we would walk three or four miles on a night as cold as last night. And hardly feel the cold because the pattern of the trees was poetry. And the moon hung in the sky; and, when we kissed, the motion of the earth paused.'

anon

I came across those words in a newspaper article in August 1962 after my first date and first kiss with my first girlfriend, Janet. To me the words were deeply relevant. We were in a world of our own, walking through the Somerset countryside under the stars. That was 55 years ago but I still recollect the time so well. We had a couple more dates although nothing matched that first spellbound evening. Janet then told me she didn't want another date, 'but we could still be friends. I was devastated. To misquote P P Arnold, the first rejection is the deepest. I wrote pleading letters to her in a forlorn attempt to persuade her to change her mind, even posting a small box of chocolates (Cadbury's Milk Tray, actually), but all this was to no avail.

We had met at the August bank holiday fairground at Clevedon. She was a good-looking girl with auburn hair, a pale face and an engaging smile. I was there with Bernard, the first male acquaintance I made on my arrival in Bristol.

Just before Christmas that same year, I was persuaded by Bernard to ride my Capri scooter to Yatton, knock on Janet's door and wish her a Happy Christmas. My stomach was churning and doing cartwheels but Bernard persisted. Reluctantly I went along with his idea and walked up the path to her house, climbing over a motorbike on the way. Her mother answered the door. I couldn't speak. She stared quizzically at me and, after a pause, looked over her shoulder and said,

'Janet, I think it's for you.'

Janet came to the door.

'Oh Chris! What a surprise! But I can't speak now, my boyfriend is here.'

Ah, I surmised, that would explain the motorbike. As I was so tongue-tied, I just gave her a half smile and turned to walk away. I could have kept some dignity if I hadn't tripped over said motorbike. Thank you, Bernard, that was a great idea!

A few years ago, I looked up Janet on 'Friends Reunited', perhaps the first social media site, now discontinued, and read her profile. She married very young, had a daughter, divorced, remarried and now lives in Norfolk.
Well, there you go.

4

BEYOND THE FIRST LOVE

I joined a bank in Bristol in 1962, initially for six weeks' training at the Totterdown branch. The branch was closed some years ago and is now a successful café bar. Some might think this a much better use of the premises.

My priority in the big city was to join a local youth club. There I could view girls up-front, although in those early days I would still not have the courage to speak to them, so was unlikely to get a date. I would, however, make good male friends who would help me build my confidence to get closer to these mysterious characters.

I met Peggy at a Sunday youth club I had joined; she was to become my first long-term girlfriend. My chat up line still needed much improvement and I was having no luck with the vast majority of girls at the club. Peggy, though, was happy to chat to me and after a couple of weeks we experienced our first date - playing records at her parents' house. What Peggy might have lacked in looks she made up for in passion. We lasted all of nine months, a lifetime for teenagers. We had a few breaks in our time together when I became bored. I was weak willed, though, as each time we broke up she would write to persuade me to stay with her. We lived only a mile apart but regularly communicated by letter, the recognized way to keep in touch.

Bernard was her boyfriend before me, meaning he and I were able to compare notes. Was that a nice thing to do? Probably not, but she would have guessed this might well happen, knowing Bernard and I were good friends.

We became a steady couple with regular cinema visits, usually ABC Whiteladies or the Orpheus at Henleaze, but also others, many others. The Orpheus still stands, as a multi-screen cinema, and although the ABC is no more, an Everyman multi-screen cinema reopened on the site on 20th May 2016. Cinema losses since then include the Gaumont on Baldwin Street, the Gaiety on the Wells Road, the King's on Old Market, Her Majesty's, Stapleton Road, the Ritz, Brislington and many more. There was also the Tatler at Old Market which showed adult movies - so I am told - sadly demolished in 1965 to make way for the Old Market and inner-city ring road development. I enjoyed also a few visits to the Scala opposite the Zetland Road junction. This establishment had a flea pit reputation but showed original films, not always available mainstream.

Back to Peggy. She had a strict father who was manager of Martins Bank in Bristol, now long gone, absorbed by Barclays in 1969. Some films might finish late in the evening and I was told by her Dad, in no uncertain terms, she had to be home by 10.30pm, even if it meant missing the end of the film. I kept to this and escorted her to her front door by the allotted time. Last chance for a kiss and a cuddle. I would smile, she would smile, and she would tell me how much she loved my dimples - not the only part of my body she noticed. If I pressed up close against her she would say,
'I can feel your nodge!'
She had made up a new name for it. Happy times on her doorstep, often interrupted by a male voice from inside the house,
'Is that you, Peggy?'

Although my relationship with her father was strained, luckily I got on well enough with her mother. I remember one Sunday we were with her Mum watching a cricket match on a field between the Portway and the River Avon, adjacent to Sea Mills. I lit up a *Rothmans King Size* and, out of politeness, started to move away. She surprised me by calling out,
'No, Chris, stay here, the smoke keeps the midges away.'

Peggy had a close friend, Vron (Veronica) and they would chat between themselves using a form of Bristol backslang, or backspeak. This sounds like a foreign language to the uninitiated. They would speak in this way when I was in their company. That was rude. After a while, I cottoned on to how they were abusing the English language but did not let on that I could, in fact, understand what they were saying. Eventually I couldn't resist the temptation to speak to them in their slang. They were shocked, and horrified I had been listening in on their girlie chat.

One warm moonlit night, Peggy and I lay in a clearing within dense shrubs on the edge of Clifton Downs, known locally as 'The Dumps'. Our clothing was loosened and we were becoming quite aroused and physically very close. I lingered. How far would she let me go? I whispered,

'I feel helpless this close to you, Peggy, if you are not ready for this, you must tell me.'

She said nothing, gently pushing me away, just in time. Or so I thought.

A couple of weeks later she mentioned she was concerned, being a few days late. Hmm, if she was concerned then I was too, very much so. If a girl became pregnant in the early 1960s, that was is, shotguns at the ready. Abortion was illegal until the 1967 Abortion Act legalised the procedure in certain circumstances.

The following Sunday I took her on a day trip to Swanage on my Lambretta, having recently upgraded from the Capri. The weather was diabolical. We returned to Bristol, almost home when on approaching Cheltenham Road Arches, rain still falling heavily, an elderly pedestrian stepped into the road causing me to brake violently, leading to scooter, myself and Peggy landing in an undignified heap on the road. I was surprisingly uninjured, but Peggy suffered a gashed leg. I felt so guilty, she was very shaken and off work for several days. Rightly I was feeling responsible for the accident, but was more concerned and worried about her comment the previous week.

I visited her at home every evening to enquire about her leg but also to learn the latest regarding her other condition. For a few days, agonising days, she reported no change. Then towards the end of the week she graphically assured me all was well. Relief all round on that score and her leg had now almost healed. At last I felt able, finally, to break from her but not without tears on both sides.

Some while later a group of us from youth club were at a dance, a good group were playing some excellent music, covers from recent chart hits. Sometime during the evening I noticed Peggy on the other side of the dance floor. I suspected she had followed me there. All worked out well though, as at the dance she met a tall lanky lad called, I discovered later, Ronald. Some weeks after this I spotted them in town, hand in hand. Silently I wished them well. I hope they made a go of it.

After Peggy my confidence was building, and I started to 'play the field'. Or, to be precise, *tried* to play the field. I will not forget the excitement of a new girl, fond memories of enchanted evenings, memories that have never left me. But it was not all to be good news.

5

MOVING ON

At the risk of humiliating myself, and after some hesitation, I have decided to include an epistle I wrote after attending a party. I must point out in my defence that when scribbling this tirade I was young, tired, emotional and very drunk. After those provisos, please read on.

'It is 1963, I am 17 years old and what I wanted at tonight's party was to have some fun with a girl. Nothing serious. I wish I knew just what girls actually want. There were plenty at the party, some I really fancied. Most were smoking and drinking, they seemed happy, laughing and dancing around their handbags and didn't seem interested in us at all. We tried our charms on them. Tonight we were unlucky but even on successful nights, with a date arranged with a new girl, it is not necessarily always good news.

'If you play for a girl, paying them attention and making them laugh, you stand a good chance of the promise of a date. Initially they spurn your advances, but if you are persistent, they might well relent. But be careful what you wish for because this success can change to something less favourable. After a while, if a relationship becomes too serious, the girl becomes a limpet rather than a catch. The boy then gets bored and it can be difficult to break away. Once she has you as her 'steady', goodbye freedom. You then yearn for the good old days, out with your mates, discussing wild ideas and hoping for a new girl come Saturday night.'

Clearly, I wasn't ready for settling down just yet.

These early years were, on the whole, great times. I was living with my parents in a lively city and had a job giving me some money to enjoy an active social life. Working at the bank helped this along, as apart from the companionship of girls in the office, Martin and Derek, who also worked there, were good fun to be with and to share experiences. We would rib each other with our little idiosyncrasies. Martin, for example, had an extreme fear of injections. If he was due a vaccination for anything, he would be worried and anxious. I would tease him and bring up the timeworn joke,

'Come on, Martin, it's only a little prick.'

'Speak for yourself!' he would reply.

An old one but we would still laugh. The male appendage, incidentally, will be making a couple of appearances, so to speak, later in this narrative.

Life was good, I had no worries apart from how to get a date with the next girl I might fancy. Always a blow to the ego to be rejected, worth the risk though, because the girl might say 'Yes'. I was getting out and about, often one-night stands, but still very enjoyable. More so, perhaps, bearing in mind my drunken rant, less chance for boredom to set in.

I would be around town most nights, invariably involving drinking in abundance; we were all much the same. My problem was suffering regular hangovers and occasionally not turning up on time for work. This was not good, as a bank employee was expected to be sober, polite and punctual at all times. The polite bit was easy, I just had problems with the sober and punctual bits. Being late was bad enough, but one such morning I was holding the keys to the vaults. Derek will recollect rushing from the bank to wake me up and collect the keys. There were many disgruntled customers that morning and I was given a formal reprimand.

I met Hayley again, 'eyes across the school hedge' Hayley, this time at close range, when our respective families met up for a show at the Bristol Hippodrome, 'Beyond the Fringe', on tour after Edinburgh. To me, her appearance was enhanced by large dark eyes with a sparkle promising so much. She and I shared the back seat of my parents' car for the journey home from the theatre, and she delighted me in a session of passionate and prolonged teenage kissing. My grandmother was also on the back seat, on the other side of Hayley from me. Apart from a startled glance or two from my dear grandmother, she didn't interrupt us. Back at my parents' house we continued our newfound friendship in the back room. My hands started to wander 'down below'. She stopped me by saying,

'I would let you, Chris, but sorry, it's not the right time.'

I hoped there might be an occasion later when it would be the right time.

A short walk from my parents' house was a notorious dance hall, Tiffany's, at The Glen, near the top of Blackboy Hill between the junction of Redland Hill and Westbury Road. The site was originally a quarry, closing around 1876.

My father was aware of this den of vice and spoke to me,

'That place is not good, Christopher, it has a certain reputation, you will not go there.'

I suppose, as I was living at home and still in my teens, Dad was entitled to lay down the law a bit. His remark, of course, fuelled my curiosity. I thought the venue can't be all that bad, so one Monday night when at a loose end I wandered up the road, on my own, to see what all the fuss was about. With trepidation I paid my entrance fee, crept into the noisy hall and looked around to see if there might be a willing girl I could chat to. All versions of the female race were present, large and small, short and tall. Lots of severely backcombed hair and beehives, fashionable hairstyles of the early 1960s.

Shortly after my arrival, two fights broke out between ageing teddy-boys, residues from the late 1950s. They were sporting the complete outfit, including winkle pickers, sideburns and hair held in place with lashings of Brylcreem. The record being played was Leroy Van Dyke's hit, 'Walk on By'. The atmosphere made me feel quite uncomfortable and, as I hadn't been able to strike up a conversation with a girl, it was my time to walk on by (nice link that) and leave in some disappointment. Nevertheless, I had expanded my knowledge of the Bristol scene. I didn't go back.

The dance hall was replaced some years ago with a BUPA private hospital. Quite a change of use.

The bank held a dinner dance every year at the Grand Hotel in Broad Street. Each year I was to have the pleasure of a different girl on my arm. An early and memorable year was a one-night stand with Debbie, a delightful girl from the office. The evening progressed well, and much as expected, until it was time at her front door to say goodnight.

I had kissed a few girls by now but Debbie's kiss was something else, leaving me almost reeling and breathless. We are still in contact to this day, now it is just a peck on the cheek when we meet. I must remind her of that unforgettable kiss she gave me that night, but I doubt she would be prepared to relive the full and deep experience. Or perhaps she might, I'm forever hopeful. How about it, Debbie?

Everything in my life was going swimmingly until my Dad retired from his Bristol management job in the tobacco industry, and decided with my mother to move to Nailsea in the Somerset countryside. Nailsea? How was living in Nailsea going to compare with the time of my life I was having in Bristol? This was not looking good and I had a word with my employer. Could they help me financially if I moved into my own accommodation? These days the response would not be helpful, but back in the Sixties banks were still paternalistic and I had no difficulty in being granted a so-called 'lodging allowance'.

It was now a short step to find a pad of my own and continue my life in the way to which I had become accustomed. Actually, this was to be better than before, as having my own place I would be able to entertain with unlimited freedom. Happy days!

And so to my first bedsit, in Edgecumbe Road, Redland. An unusual spelling of the road, I thought. My only bedsit, actually, as after a couple of years I moved into a flat. Very little furniture was provided in the tiny bedsit beyond a sagging bed, a wonky chair, a sink and a grimy gas hob. But it was a fair rent, i.e. very cheap.

I wanted something comfy to relax on, apart from the bed. A hunt through the classified ads in the Bristol Evening Post discovered a two-seater sofa in

Westbury Park going for £2. There was no way I could afford a van so, with the help of a couple of mates, we collected the sofa and wheeled it down the road to my bedsit, a distance of a mile or so. This caused some amusement to passers-by.

'What are you doing?', they asked.

'We're moving this down to my bedsit.'

'Want a hand?'

'Thanks, that would be great.'

It was a heavy sofa. With extra hands on board we could now gather speed and all went well until two castors broke off. This changed the escapade into a real challenge, and carrying the sofa up the stairs to my bedsit even more so. Nonetheless we made it, and the sofa, in spite of being short of two castors, turned out to be a very comfortable investment.

Shortly after moving into the bedsit, a new development - Derek, with another colleague, John, moved into a double bedsitting room on the floor below me. This was a useful arrangement: as Derek and I both worked at Avonmouth, he was on hand to ensure I woke up in time. John was able to walk to his job at Durdham Down.

On our first Christmas in the house we held a party, with our landlord's consent. We invited willing girls from the bank and a good time was had by all. Actually, a very good time. Until now I had always considered Derek to be a fairly conservative sort of chap on that front. That's as maybe, but he did enjoy himself at the party that night.

I had many diverse and varied encounters at Edgecumbe Road, including receiving a surprising letter from Angie, the girlfriend of a chap I knew who had best remain nameless. I will call him Mark. I still have the letter:

'Dear Chris, Me and Mark have a problem and we thought you could perhaps help us solve it. I expect you've already jumped to the conclusion we sleep together. Well it's quite true that we do - when we get the opportunity. That's where you come in - if you were to invite us to your place one evening and give us a couple of hours, we'd be very grateful. I know it's an awful cheek but he wouldn't ask you so I decided I would. Please help, Ange.'

What frustrates me is I cannot recall whether or not I agreed to her rather outlandish request. 'Mark' cannot remember either, although he does remember the girl. A bit of a tart, apparently, but in his words, a tasty tart.

We arrived at our second Christmas at Edgecumbe Road and, after the success of the previous party, decided to repeat the experience. First item on the agenda was to confirm the landlord would be happy for us to hold another party. He was not. It must have been an excellent, if noisy, festive occasion the previous year. But entertainment on alternative fronts was to be not far away.

6

YOUTH CLUBS

Youth clubs were ideal venues to get to know girls. Some might feel that now, at the great age of 17 years, I would be past belonging to such clubs. In the two I joined, both linked to churches, most of the lads were of a similar age; some of the girls were a little younger. I made several lasting friendships over the ensuing years.

None of us could be called fashionable in the clothing department. The early Sixties were before the flower power era, so neither boys nor girls would be wearing flowers in their hair. I had one special item of clothing, a brown mohair pullover purchased from a department store in Broadmead. It does sound naff now but I thought it was the pinnacle of high fashion.

There were other examples of the time. Footwear of choice away from work would be either daps (trainers) or Hush Puppies, also known as brothel creepers: why they were so called I know not but perhaps owing to their rubber soles were very quiet. Carnaby Street and all it entailed was not to arrive until later.

By now I was well into visiting pubs and consuming quantities of beer. On those nights with a shortage of girls at the Sunday night youth club to chat to, a few of us might wander down the road to the local hostelry, the Post Office Tavern. It has kept the name to this day, unlike some pub owners who cannot resist a name change, often to something naff. Here at the Tavern we would enjoy pints of brown split (Georges bitter and brown ale) or occasionally sweet cider, but not the genuine stuff which was to be found only in the cider houses in the city, or deep in the Somerset countryside.

The landlord at the Tavern, a nice enough chap on the surface, had two teenage daughters. I never met the girls but others apparently did have the pleasure. He once spoke to us,

'Any bloke can do whatever he likes with either of my daughters provided he takes care.'

Was this a sign that the permissive Sixties was on the horizon?

After a while even visits to the pub became a tad boring. On the route between the youth club and the pub was a private girls' school (it's still there). Some bright spark suggested it might be fun to creep into the grounds of the school 'to see what we can see'. Nothing, as it turned out, and as we were caught the second time undertaking this escapade, our night-time prowling was short lived.

These activities were all set in a rather posh part of Bristol and the girls at the youth club tended to be well educated, some attending the convent school adjacent to the church. One such girl, an early experience for me, was Julie, a young vivacious lass with long sleek dark hair, very attractive in a 'girl next door' sort of way. I enjoyed a couple of dates with her. These events were quite innocent apart from one evening when I did try my luck and moved to fondle her breasts. There was nothing there. Sixteen years old, petite, and still to develop in that direction.

In her later years she married a carpenter and produced seventeen children, quite a feat for such a diminutive girl. Articles appeared in the national press, together with photos of the family. So that was Julie, a good Catholic girl. A lucky escape for me, she was a delight, but seventeen children? Would I have cherished that? I think not, an intriguing thought though, all the same.

The church to which the Sunday night youth club was linked built a splendid church hall, Newman Hall. This was completed in 1962 and became an excellent venue for theatre and dance; proper dances with a band. We had a much-loved routine which comprised half a dozen of us in a row performing

'Freddie's Dance'. We would be mimicking the celebrated stage act of Freddie and the Dreamers, a popular Liverpudlian group.

We were regulars at another church youth club, held on a Thursday evening. Adjacent to this club was again a church hall with a bar, frequented by a large local Irish contingent. Invariably, the bar staff refused to serve us, so it was down to Mrs Miggins Teashop on Gloucester Road. I never knew if that was her real name but that's what we called her. There we would enjoy weak milky coffee served in those cheap, almost saucer shaped, thick glass coffee cups. The high life indeed.

We were generally law abiding but, even so, involved ourselves in some inauspicious moments. Being teenagers, we were not immune from getting into mischief and we did not always behave with decorum. One November 5th night I will not forget, indeed I am embarrassed when I am reminded of the event.

A group of us from the Thursday youth club drifted around the city centre and suburbs letting off bangers. I know, not very original. Small ones cost one old penny, the tuppenny bangers were better value giving a much bigger bang. All great fun until we were chased by a publican - in his car. We escaped but it was a close shave. The adventure became known as 'The Stapleton Road incident'.

We didn't repeat the experience.

We were always on the lookout for somewhere different to spend our evenings as a change from our regular youth clubs. We heard about a club in lower Clifton, 'The Ninepins'. Nothing to do with skittles, just another youth club with a Dansette record player and a soft drinks bar. The club was dominated by a couple of fairly beefy lads who seemed to spend their time walking round the clubroom, puffing out their chests. One of our group who shall remain nameless (alright, it was Brendan) muttered,

'O yea, really hard.'

Big mistake. The gang leader came over to us and snarled,

'Hard? We'll show you who's hard.'

Within seconds we were knocked from our chairs, Brendan received a bit of a bashing and my glasses were broken in the scuffle. We bid a hasty retreat and, unsurprisingly, did not return.

7

DOWN TOWN

So, Sundays and Thursdays were youth club nights which left five nights a week for girlfriends or to go out on the town with male company. It was quite normal to be out most nights, but Saturday was the night for looking for girls. Often this would be with Mike or Bernard from the Sunday youth club. A line from 'I Get Around' by the Beach Boys springs to mind:

'None of the guys go steady cause it wouldn't be right to leave their best girl home on a Saturday night.'

Bristol suffered badly during the Bristol Blitz of 1940/41 with heavy bombing and many buildings badly damaged or destroyed. Broadmead was redeveloped during the 1950s but there was still much to do, with wartime damage evident throughout the city. As part of the continued redevelopment, Mecca Leisure Group built the Bristol Entertainment Centre, an ugly monstrosity officially named The New Bristol Centre, at a cost of £2 million. Unfortunately, this action entailed the destruction of another little part of Bristol history, although thankfully the historic Hatchet Inn was saved after a determined local campaign. The Centre was at the time the largest entertainment complex in Europe. Included in the development was the Bristol Ice Rink which became a popular venue for meeting members of the opposite sex.

It was on the ice I met the first of several Susans. This first Susan was a particularly charming girl with shoulder length blonde hair and delightful facial expressions when she laughed. Her father owned an independent estate agency on Stokes Croft. She was a considerably better ice skater then me; that would not have been difficult. Our association was short, more's the pity: she soon dumped me.

There were times I felt uncomfortable phoning a girl at her home in case one of her parents answered, and I might be quizzed by them and have to explain my motives. As this was well before mobile phones or the internet, to make contact and keep parents out of the equation, we would as a rule correspond in the customary way by handwritten letter, as I mentioned earlier. I did write to Susan in an attempt to re-establish our time together, this resulting in a singularly unsuccessful outcome. I was not downhearted as, in my optimism, I felt sure in time I would meet someone else. I did not have long to wait for new alliances, but it was to be a while before being blessed with another long-term girlfriend.

The next step in my quest was to enrol for dancing tuition. Dancing with a girl during a lesson was the natural thing to do, there being no danger of being rejected.

Beginners night at a favourite dance studio in Clifton was often successful for meeting girls. On my first night there I met Deborah. She was a quiet girl who sported an amazing crop of dishevelled dark hair. I would engineer my way around the dance floor to maximise my chances of dancing with her.

She let me walk her home on a number of occasions and even let me hold her delicate soft hand. This might not sound much now but it set my heart a-fluttering. Again, this relationship, if it could be called that, did not last long. I suspect her parents had something to do with it; she was probably quite young. The lyrics to Gary Puckett's 1968 hit, 'Young Girl', could be appropriate:

> *Young girl, get out of my mind*
> *My love for you is way out of line*
> *Better run girl*
> *You're much too young, girl*

Mike and I enrolled for the beginners class at the dance studio for three years running. In year two, we could have proceeded quite easily to the intermediate level but reckoned opportunities were better, for our intentions, at the entry stage. On the first night of our second enrolment, the organiser suspected she had seen us before. On the first night of our *third* enrolment she exclaimed,

'You again! How can you still be beginners?'

We might have been guilty of leading her to question her abilities as a dance instructor.

Another girl I met at the dance studio was Penny, a well-spoken and cultivated young lady, not surprising qualities perhaps, considering she was being educated at the private girls' school referred to earlier. 15-years-old, Penny was two years younger than me, or so she led me to believe; not too big an age difference, I figured. But shock and horror, I found out later from an ally of hers - Moira - that Penny was only 13-years-old. Thirteen? No way! I was fond of young girls but not that young, I was no Jimmy Saville. A reminder of Gary Puckett's lyrics again. All the more embarrassing for me as my mates milked the story for all it was worth. Luckily it had been a platonic friendship.

Once I had learnt her age, I didn't see her again, which was a shame as we had arranged a date and she was going to let me have a photo of herself. I still remember her appearance, slightly taller than me and slim, a pretty girl and I insist she looked at least 15 years of age…

A popular club, later in the Sixties, was The Mandrake, a cellar bar and discotheque (the description of such venues not yet shortened to 'disco') in Frogmore Street, in the centre of Bristol just opposite the previously mentioned Hatchet Inn. The club, by the way, was relaunched in 2009 as Basement 45 and is still in business. There was a long waiting list for men. Still, we put our names down and eventually became members.

We were frequent visitors for the first couple of weeks until one weekend Douglas, who I knew from youth club, turned up from London, where he now lived. Douglas was known as Mac in view of his surname - McCann. He was keen to join us at the club but was not a member and nor was he keen to pay the heavy entrance fee levied on a guest. Mac had this cunning plan.

Those of us who were members would go in first. A little later in the evening, Mac would turn up, pretending to be me, explaining regretfully he had left his membership card at home. This seemed like a good plan, but we had not allowed for the club owner on the door having a photographic memory. She knew I was already in the club and sent her bouncers to escort me from the building. In silence she relieved me of my membership card and refunded my joining fee of £4.4/- (£4.20) in full, which I did not expect. But small consolation for my association being terminated so soon after barely three weeks. It was a great club and I was well pissed off.

Much later, with a new owner on the door, I would be signed in as a guest, but I did regard my earlier experience as a humiliation. I will mention later how certain pop hits recollect incidents in my life. During my eviction from The Mandrake the DJ was playing 'Love Grows (Where My Rosemary Goes)', by the London band Edison Lighthouse, and whenever I hear the track now, I am reminded of that unfortunate, and embarrassing, episode in my life.

Nights wandering the centre of Bristol were too frequently a washout. The highlight of the evening might be a greasy hot dog or burger bought from one of the street mobile units (run by Unger & Co. of St. Pauls).

'You like des onions?'

'Yes please, onions with both, thank you'.

A hot dog and a couple of pints of Georges bitter and we would still have change from ten bob (50p). We were not big spenders, we didn't have the cash. Sadly, Mr Unger's business is no more, no doubt a victim of environmental health issues. We relished and enjoyed his products on many a night in town with no unpleasant surprises.

Bristol gives her name to a part of a woman's anatomy, or rather two parts. Everyone has heard of 'Bristols'. What is less commonly known is the origin of the term which is, apparently, rhyming slang as in Bristol City - titty. To quote one of my heroes, 'Not many people know that'.

Bristol girls come in many shapes and sizes as they do anywhere else, of course. They were sometimes called 'dolly-birds' (how dated is that?) but they were not all necessarily 'nice' girls. Certainly some we saw, particularly in the city centre on a Saturday night, could not be considered demure or modest, or be the sort of girl one might take home to meet the parents.

Some were not shy in their vocabulary. One such girl was in a large group, I guess a hen party, and had a slogan emblazoned across the front of her t-shirt, 'Any cock'le do'. Nice. We avoided her; well, I did. Then there was the scantily dressed tipsy girl tottering on her high heels we overheard say,

'I need a pee but can't be fagged to pull me knickers down.'

I contemplated how this might have worked out. Yes, always plenty of rough down town but not for us (unless we were *really* desperate).

Evenings in town would often end with walking home for an inquest into another unsuccessful evening. A massive hit for the 'Stones' at the time was '(I Can't Get No) Satisfaction'. Although a double negative, I do understand perfectly well what Mick meant and the title often matched our despondent mood.

On one fruitless night with Mike we drowned our sorrows and, with Dutch courage, broke into song; this was unusual for us. We started walking home, first up Park Street and, as we approached

Triangle South, we stepped into the middle of the road (less traffic in the 1960s) and sang at the tops of our voices 'All My Loving' by The Beatles. I have no idea what prompted that. Apart from the beer.

Arriving home after a futile trip down town we would discuss our love life, or lack of it, reflecting on past assignations. We might perhaps have seen an 'ex' in town and conversation might become somewhat down-to-earth.

One such discussion did not involve me, but Mike and Bernie (not Bernard, but another male friend with a very similar name) who I had recently met at the Sunday youth club. One night, they were in Bernie's parents' house having a conversation and apparently not holding back on graphic detail in describing their exploits. Unfortunately, the house was not noted for effective sound proofing. Bernie was approached by his Dad the following morning with,

'We don't like being woken up in the early hours with the 2 o'clock news. Keep the details of your sordid love life to yourselves.'

There were good nights and bad nights down town, we always lived in eternal hope. 'We'll be lucky tonight'. We could cope with those dark, dismal and depressing evenings (not that I want to sound too negative) as there was always likely to be another time which might be one of those captivating nights we would never forget. And there were a few of those.

Let me digress briefly to comment on the Bristol pub scene.

I'll drink to that

In 1960, the city was blessed with several hundred public houses. I revelled in visiting many of them, some sadly no more. There was a wide choice of rough and ready serious drinking houses. Others would be the place to take your girl on a date, pubs such as the Lamb and Flag at Cribbs Causeway, and other classier pubs slightly out of town, a popular haunt being the Jolly Sailor at Saltford. Not many so-called gastro pubs then.

Some pubs famously live on, such as the Llandoger Trow in King Street, originally famed for a wide selection of sherries in addition to ales. Many city pubs are linked to the glory days when Bristol was a major port - evocative names from Bristol's seafaring history, such as the Hope and Anchor, the Naval Volunteer and the Nova Scotia.

Other pubs include the Assize Courts, named because the Bristol Crown Court was nearby. The Old Duke in the docks, some say named in honour of Duke Ellington, is still renowned today for jazz and blues. Other pubs had a certain reputation: The Hatchet, for instance, but this is now a respected hostelry hosting rock music upstairs. And then the Three Tuns on St. George's Road, traditionally a notorious rough joint; you wouldn't take your girl there. The pub is different now, being a well-run real ale establishment.

The Lamplighters on the river below Shirehampton goes way back. The recognised reason for the pub being so named was to honour a local man whose occupation was to light the many oil lamps in the surrounding suburbs. I like to think he would also light, although unlikely, the lamps which are still positioned along the River Avon to assist vessels navigating to and from the city docks.

Not much traffic on the river now, but the lamps have survived. There was even a passenger ferry - by way of a rowing boat - between the Lamplighters and the village of Pill on the other side of the river.

Another example of Bristol history was lost when the ferry closed in 1974, caused by loss of business following the opening of the Avonmouth bridge.

8

THE SWINGING SIXTIES

This was a special era. The Swinging Sixties, the permissive society, whatever, was a unique time for a boy or a girl but not always quite as might be imagined. In the early Sixties sexual liberation was on the horizon, and getting closer, although often still just a topic of conversation rather than actually being practiced.

The contraceptive pill was available from around 1964 though only for married women, and only then after an intrusive inquisition for the poor lady. There was still plenty of heated activity going on, but also a good deal of innocence. I came across examples of both.

There was one girl of note I did not date, too young for me, but I learnt she had what I considered an unusual arrangement at home. Her mother was divorced and, knowing her 13-year-old daughter was quite promiscuous and sexually active, agreed to swop her double bed for her daughters' single. Her mother was heard to say,

'If she's going down that path let it be here at home where I can keep an eye on her and on whoever she is with, rather than somewhere else.'

She had a point, but I was not convinced a girl that young should be encouraged in such a way. Not merely because it was illegal, more that the girl would have little to anticipate in the future, when older. I do agree it was a quandary for this particular mother, though.

In those early days we had not heard of oral sex as such, although we might have been tempted to investigate tentatively with a peep, and possibly more, down below. Taken further, that particular practice has a name, cunnilingus. We would not have known that: we do now, thank you Michael Douglas.

One of many pleasing aspects of living throughout the 1960s was the emergence of the mini skirt. How nice was that! This form of attire was not limited to evening wear but also worn at work. The young girls (well, most of them) and a few older ladies would show off their legs. And thighs. The mini skirt era and then, for a while, a fashion for hot pants ensured many happy days for the male population.

Christmas Eve and New Year's Eve were good for taking liberties, and we would make the most of opportunities as they arose. Young men will behave the same today. It was that time of the year when revellers lost their inhibitions. Rich opportunities indeed for horny young men in Bristol. One particular Christmas Eve is embedded in the memory.

A group of us were walking past the Corn Exchange on our way to the Rummer, a very old established cellar bar in Bristol, for our next pint, when we passed a column of girls walking in the opposite direction. Except we didn't walk straight past. Each boy kissed each girl in turn, quickly but passionately. A performance with similarities, perhaps, to two football teams shaking hands with each other prior to a match. We never saw the girls again - as far as we know. It was not in our minds to slow our progress to the pub by stopping to take note of names and addresses.

That night was also notable for another reason. Later, we were making our way towards Clifton when, suddenly, I needed to throw up. We were passing a building site where I emptied my stomach and bladder, then my stomach again. I lay down for a brief rest, at least that was the intention, and closed my eyes. I did not wake until the dawn of Christmas Day, bitterly cold. Where were my mates? Surely we were not in such a large group they didn't miss me?

On another Christmas Eve one of our group, Richard, was told by his parents, without

43

warning, to leave home, not just to return to university but to leave for good. He was 19-years-old and did leave, never to return. He stayed with me for a while until he sorted out something more permanent. His parents never relented. I was never sure of the exact cause of the rift although it might have had something to do with him cohabiting with his girlfriend Maggie at university (quite normal now, not so then). Also, his parents were outwardly devout Christians and pillars of local society. Richard getting another girl pregnant on holiday in Morocco might not have helped the relationship. Certainly, he did his bit to support the permissive society.

I *also* left home while still a teenager, 17-years-old in my case, but that was with my parents' agreement and probably their blessing.

Richard had a chequered life and sadly died of a heart attack soon after his 50th birthday. His widowed mother did at least have the decency to attend his funeral.

I mentioned the mini skirt earlier. Tights were rare during the Sixties until this new revealing garment emerged around 1965. Tights then became a necessity to replace stockings and so to avoid an exposed suspender gap, but this development was not good news for us blokes. If a girl was wearing stockings, there was that wonderful sensation (at least for us if not for the girl) of running a hand up the girls' thigh, feeling for the bare flesh, moving inside the knickers and if no objections were made perhaps beyond, being guided by early evidence of an emerging undergrowth, depending on how well the girl was developing. A 'Brazilian' is popular today, gratefully not then. This hand manoeuvre became quite a daunting challenge when tights were encountered.

On this subject, I was once told a story by a vague acquaintance of the night he picked up a girl at the Top Rank Ballroom, took her home to his bedsit and was hoping to have, if not his evil way with her, at least a bit of fun. He started the usual struggle with her tights when she volunteered,

'No need for that, I 'ave an 'ole in me tights, you'll find what you're looking for down there.'

As I said, Bristol did have its' fair share of rough.

First dates. Some were the epitome of innocence, some were steamy and moist. On one hand there was affectionate Gina, a sweet girl, but she allowed no more than a peck on the cheek on our first date. She was a nurse at Ham Green Hospital, now long gone, who wanted to become a Catholic and was a very good girl. This was not what I was looking for. By chance my mother, an auxiliary nurse at the hospital, met Gina there and was so impressed, said to me,

'You must invite her out again Christopher, she is a really nice girl.'

She *was* a nice girl, but I was looking more for a naughty girl. I didn't have long to wait.
Shortly after Gina I met Lena, a similar name but there the similarity ends. I took her to the Orpheus

Cinema at Henleaze on our first date. Quite a good film, Peter Sellers in 'Only Two Can Play'. Time to settle into our seats, arm around her shoulder, free hand moving over her petite breasts, only for Lena to move aforementioned hand down to between her legs which she then pressed against her pride, and my joy. And she was wearing a micro mini skirt. I was taken aback, surprised and startled. A wanton woman! Just what I've been waiting for! I continued with what I believed she wanted me to do, but discreetly, we were not in the back row.

The explanation for her enthusiasm might have been caused by her being a convent schoolgirl. Being repressed at school she perhaps went overboard when away from the stern gaze of Mother Superior. Mind you, Lena did hail from New Zealand, so perhaps was interested in all things *down under*...

That word, *moist*, I mentioned earlier. A recent survey revealed the word is one of the most disliked in the English language. Not by me, as it is a reminder of those steamy sessions of my youth. Groin is another word giving pleasurable thoughts and I'm not thinking of what you might find on a beach. And thrusting... No, I must stop now.

9

SCOOTER WORLD

I was a scooter fan since my arrival in Bristol and was keen to start a club - for two reasons. I wanted to meet like-minded riders and I suspected, rightly as it turned out, this could be another avenue leading towards new opportunities.

Before I moved to my bedsit, I wrote a letter to the Evening Post suggesting that if anyone else out there might be interested in starting such a club, they should join me outside the Victoria Rooms the following Saturday at 10.30am. Five others turned up and we rode to my parents' house, noisily, for our inaugural meeting. I was *most* unpopular with my dad. We chose a name, the Harlequins, and found club premises at the Pineapple Inn behind the Council House, as it was then known, on College Green. The pub sadly closed some years ago and is about to be converted into another block of flats.

Initially, I had not realised there were already four such clubs in Bristol so we soon merged with the thriving and successful Bristol Eagle Scooter Club.

We were a well organised group with a properly run membership and a code of conduct. In common with other clubs, we designed our very own leg-shield banner, including our logo, which members were entitled to buy and fit across the front of their machines. We took this a stage further by also using the same logo on a cloth badge to be sown on the front of a members' leather jacket. I still have mine. The badge that is, not the jacket.

The design of the logo was copied almost exactly from the *Eagle* logo of Barclays Bank, but we were not pursued by them which I considered surprising. At our peak we had well over 100 members driving around Bristol, sporting the logo. Perhaps Barclays saw this as free advertising and were happy to let us get on with it. I doubt it though.

So, as I had surmised, being a member of the club opened up a whole new world of activities appealing to me. Not for nothing was I keen to be in a club attracting young ladies. They could be quite forward in their manner but I would not call them groupies, they were not promiscuous. Well, perhaps a few might have been...

Some of the girls did not possess a machine of their own and would be on the lookout for pillion rides on weekend club runs. A girl riding pillion sometimes needed educating as to how a two-wheeled machine should be handled. There were times a girl, new to scootering, might climb on behind me, but on the first corner of the journey would lean in the opposite direction to me. Most disconcerting, but once educated, it was nice to have a girl holding me close and tightly, albeit perhaps through fear rather than affection.

Club runs were to Weymouth and the like. Brighton was receiving media attention, being the resort of choice for mods and rockers: we never considered ourselves to be either. That resort was a fair trek from Bristol, so for us it was routinely Weymouth.

Our outings were properly organised with a Run Leader and two 'Tail End Charlies' who would mop up stragglers, usually caused by breakdowns, of which there were many. We were generally a polite and well-mannered lot but when we set up camp around our totem pole on Weymouth beach, we were given a wide berth by other beach users.

The club venue tended to change from time to time and was usually based in a room over a pub. Club nights were great fun with beer for the lads and lager and lime, or Babycham, for the girls, a healthy mix of the sexes and a common love of scootering. Just one club night was the exception to this happy environment - the day President Kennedy was assassinated, 22nd November 1963. We were numb that night, many of the girls were crying. It is said most people remember where they were when hearing the news. I certainly do.

Babycham, incidentally, is similar to cider but made with pears instead apples, and was invented by Francis Showering of Shepton Mallet in 1953. It became a popular drink during the 1960s. It was originally sold in two-pint flagons. Sales were uninspiring until Showering had the inspiration to sell the drink in miniature bottles, call it Champagne Perry and substantially increase the price. This was coupled with an advertising campaign featuring 'Bambi', the baby deer featured in the 1942 Walt Disney film of the same name. Ah bless. Sales went through the roof and Showering's profits followed.

I said we were well mannered and we were, apart from one objectionable club member, Clive, who was a bully, confrontational and arrogant. He also refused to pay his club dues, and this irritated me as I was club treasurer (no escaping this role being the only bank employee in the club).

One warm evening, most members were chatting outside the latest club premises in Royal York Crescent, enjoying the fine weather, when Clive, for no apparent reason, picked a fight with a passing stranger. Wrong decision, Clive. He was severely beaten up.

Our accommodation in the magnificent Royal York Crescent was our most ambitious club base, and so much more than just a room over a pub. We leased the entire ground floor of a property near the junction with Wellington Crescent. This gave us space for the clubroom, committee room, and even a workshop. Sadly, our days were numbered as the established clientele in the vicinity did not take kindly to swarms of scooters littering their road. They petitioned the council and we were evicted, resulting in a front-page story in the Evening Post. Many Bristolians were on our side, but we were no match for the suits at the Council House.

Now those young ladies: ok, one or two might not have been totally respectable. We didn't hold that against them as they made delightful company, all good fun to have around and sufficiently broad-minded. Daisy and Buttercup (what were their real names?) both owned yellow Vespas, and each had their nickname emblazoned across the side panels of their scooter. Two diminutive blondes, but dumb they were not. They would give the impression of being up for anything. Unhappily this wasn't the case, at least not with me, but perhaps others had better luck.

The quietly spoken Irene was special, as I shared her with Don, the club secretary. An unusual practice, perhaps, but the three of us were well aware of the situation and quite content with the arrangement. That is, until she dumped us both.
In our heyday the club was one of the largest in the UK. Apart from Sunday club runs, we organised a

wide range of activities including barbecues on Portishead beach - the girls loved those - dances at the ABC Whiteladies ballroom, navigation trials and rallies.

One such navigation trial was around Somerset and I had the pleasure of a girl riding pillion. It did not take long for me to become disorientated and hopelessly lost. Then darkness descended. The girl was not interested in taking advantage of the isolated location and correctly blamed me for our predicament. Not my finest hour.

As I indicated earlier, scooters were not known for their reliability, to a large extent due to the age of the machines. It would be a very rare member who could afford to buy new. Lambrettas were my preferred choice, but they were just as likely to let me down as other makes.

One particular machine died in the centre of Bristol the day after I had laid out hard earned cash on its purchase. I pushed the wretched appliance all the way back to Redland. Half way home I again attempted to coax it back into life whereupon, to add to my misery, the kick-start fell off. No electric ignition in those days.

I have never had any ability as a mechanic and shall always be most indebted to my friends for their admirable assistance with my breakdowns and repairs.

Between owning Lambrettas, I had the great misfortune to possess a 250cc BSA Sunbeam, a sort of cross between a scooter and a motorbike. Much of my wages were spent on repairs.

The most notable memory of the diabolical machine was a near death experience. One damp evening I was riding along Hotwell Road (often incorrectly referred to as Hotwells Road). I was aware my headlamp was flickering; there were few parts of the bike not malfunctioning. Ahead of me was a tanker waiting to pull across in front of me into a filling station. The driver took my erratic headlamp beam to be indicating I was flashing him to pull out. Which he did. I ended up on the tarmac but fortunately not under the wheels of the tanker which I avoided by inches. Immediately I sold the bike at a substantial loss which did not concern me; I was not prepared to risk my life again.

I stayed as a member of the club well after I had progressed to my first car. For a year or two, I was the proud owner of both a Lambretta TV175, which replaced the Sunbeam, and a 1959 Austin A40 purchased for £210 with the help of a car loan from my dad. Ok, I could have applied for a loan from my employers but they would charge me interest. I was a poorly paid bank clerk and needed all the financial help I could get.

The Lambretta helped me keep in touch with the club and the enjoyable female company. The hopes and expectations of further opportunities were too good to pass by. I was a scooter man at heart and, although now owning a car, I continued to enjoy scootering around Bristol for some time to come.

I enjoyed immensely my scooter days, but it could be a cold and wet life. Apart from a car being warmer and usually drier, there are certain activities one can get up to in a car that would be quite impractical sitting on a scooter.

10

BANKING OPPORTUNITIES

I hasten to point out I am not referring to career opportunities here. Working in a bank where the majority of staff and many customers were female, gave me an advantage compared to being employed elsewhere. Indeed, Mike mentioned recently to me he was a little envious of my situation. His prospects with the ladies were limited in his field, the chemical industry, being surrounded by mostly male scientists. Mind you, not all employees there were male, and he did find opportunities later on...

After my initial training at Totterdown, I was based at the Avonmouth branch of the bank for some years. We worked very well as a team and developed an enviable camaraderie. The older men, including the manager, chief clerk and principal cashier are no longer with us. A few of us who are still around meet up for an annual reunion, nothing fancy, just a pub lunch in a Somerset hostelry.

In my early years at Avonmouth, I delighted in various short-term flirtations before developing more serious liaisons which I cover later. One girl of note was Jan, the office supervisor, a little older than me. I was very keen on her but she would act 'hard to get'. This was frustrating until at her 21st birthday party we kissed for the first time. Doesn't sound like a big thing now, but as I mentioned earlier, in my youth a first kiss with a new girl was always special, a magical moment. I was in heaven while it lasted, both that prolonged first kiss and our ensuing dates.

These were happy times and so much happier than my school days. It is said 'School days, the happiest days of your life'. I don't think so, not for me, thank you very much. Now working, I was able to enjoy new challenges, and not necessarily all relating to young ladies.

In winter there was the trial of lighting the office boiler for heating. Oh joy. This task fell to Derek or myself, usually Derek, as he had the knack. He coined a phrase 'I'll do it all' which we were to hear ad nauseam, but we loved him for it.

Derek was always one for a practical joke. He once gave me a message to phone a Mr. C. Lyon. I dialled the number:

'Good morning, Bristol Zoo. Can I help you?'

I had overlooked it was April 1st.

Then, who amongst the staff could forget the lasting memory of the principal cashier, Mr. Ralls, emptying his pipe into the wicker paper basket, causing an office fire.

Less exciting activities in the job included coping with bank inspectors. Like many others at that time, I had a so-called 'Beatles' haircut. I was told in no uncertain terms by one visiting inspector:

'Mr. Walker, get yourself a neat and proper haircut commensurate with working in a bank. If you don't get yourself sorted out, mark my words, your career will suffer.'

To make such a comment today is unlikely to be tolerated and would, no doubt, be classified as an infringement of the individual's rights.

At Avonmouth, Susan from Lennard's shoe shop next door paid in the daily shop takings. Another Susan. So many Susans, why couldn't parents try to name their daughters something more imaginative? Something inspiring like say Fanny, as in Fanny Craddock? Or Pussy, after Pussy Galore? Not only very attractive names but descriptive too, and undoubtedly feminine. I know Fanny was popular in the 'olden days', perhaps not Pussy. I did once meet a young girl called Fanny but I have never met a Pussy.

Anyway, the Lennard's Susan. One day I was manning the number 2 till, alongside Mr. Ralls. Hoping for a date, I chatted her up, at length, over the banking counter until I was given a right ticking off by the chief clerk. In my desire to impress the girl, I was oblivious to the queue of increasingly irate customers building up behind her. To use an expression of the day, a bonny lass, and I took her as pillion on a couple of club runs to Weymouth. All fairly platonic; she was a nice girl.

I commented earlier on the paternalistic nature of the bank in the 1960s. That had advantages as we were valued and cared for, but the chief clerk at Avonmouth thought it his duty to go further and do his bit to safeguard our morals, in particular *my* morals. One lunchtime I was minding my own business, eating my sandwiches in the staff rest room and reading a paperback, 'The Flesh is Weak', based on the book by Gilbert Miller. I had seen the 'X' certificate film. Gordon saw what I was reading, put his hand on my shoulder and in a raised voice barked,

'Mr. Walker, I never want to see you reading that sort of objectionable trash, put it away now, preferably in the bin.'

I took the book home to read at my leisure, uninterrupted.

The office facilities very basic with a single unisex loo and a cramped rest room. When I became a car owner, I preferred to go out for lunch and would drive to the Shirehampton chippy for fish and chips, to be eaten in a layby off the Portway. I was putting on weight - too many chips - and would loosen my trousers for comfort and listen to the transistor radio on the back seat.

Fitted car radios were a luxury. I would lose myself in my thoughts and day dreams, listening to the early days of pirate radio. Radio London was my favourite but Radio Caroline was the most well-known.

On one such day, returning to the office, I noticed our latest recruit, lovely 16-year-old innocent Mary Lush - her real name - a girl blessed with exquisite blonde hair down to her waist. Derek nicknamed her 'Scraggs' which was a bit unfair as her hair was always perfect with not a strand out of place. She was struggling with the NCR adding machine. Here was a gifted opportunity to get close and personal with this stunning girl. I leant over her to see if I could help. This resulted in a piercing scream from the young Mary. After my fish and chip lunch I had fastened my belt but forgot to pull up my fly, and the end of my shirt tail was peeping out. It was my good fortune nothing else was peeping out. I never did manage a date with Mary.

I will not forget Vicky, unkindly called by others 'Sticky Vicky', the assistant at Frost's tobacconist just around the corner. An affectionate girl with few inhibitions, and I felt we were inventing a new form of heavy petting. But of course, there's nothing new under the sun. One morning at work, after a hot and torrid date with Vicky the night before, Derek commented,

'You must have had some fun last night with that love bite on your neck.'

Horror! I had no idea what a love bite was. I told him I banged my neck servicing my scooter. He didn't believe me.

By now I was cottoning on to one of the reasons for my spasmodic success with girls. They must think if I worked in a bank, I must have good prospects. I am sure it wasn't for my looks. My four years at Avonmouth were full of new discoveries and I felt my life could not be bettered. More was to come, not only successes but failures and disappointments too.

11

KAREN

Petite, but well formed

Thanks to my job, I met my second long term girlfriend, Karen. For quite some time I was the cashier at the Shirehampton sub office of the bank. She was a cashier at the local sub Post Office. (In 2016 this office was dramatically blown up in an ATM raid).

Karen's job included paying into the bank the takings of the previous day. I met a few girls this way. A chatty girl, diminutive, slim with short blonde hair and with her approachable manner, some might say forward, I suffered no awkwardness in asking her for a date. This would be preferable to just chatting over the counter, our only interaction so far. I asked for a date. She laughed and replied,

'I'd love to!'

I must have tickled her fancy. If not then, I would try later, during some of our more intimate moments.

Her diminutive stature caused not a little discomfort for the 67-year-old guard. A guard was a bank requirement if there was only one member of staff in attendance at a sub office, but there was no limitation on the age of the guard. Charlie admitted to me that one day, in a grandfatherly manner, he welcomed Karen into the bank with an affectionate arm around her waist, quite a natural thing to do in the circumstances. Except he had not allowed for her height; he had inadvertently wrapped his arm around her breasts. I joked,

'Ok, for you, Charlie, I would never have dared do that, not in the office!'

He was *very* embarrassed.

I worked at the Shirehampton sub-office for a couple of years and established a daily routine, from opening up in the morning until closing at the end of the day. With Charlie I then caught the bus back to the parent branch at Avonmouth. Invariably, or so it seemed to me, I would be standing in the queue next to this randy young gentleman who invariably had his trousers loosened and his tongue way down his girlfriend's throat. I had to look the other way.

Looking back on some of the girls with whom I experienced more than just a one-night stand, Janet was my first love, brief but very dear, Peggy was passionate, Vicky rather more so, and others could be sometimes cool, sometimes hot. Karen, however, was something else. We were not into pubs, meals out or even walking, more into each other. She taught me a lot about what girls have down there and she learnt, or probably already knew, how to arouse a boy. We were 'going out' but in practice more likely to be 'staying in'.

Most evenings were spent either at my place or at her parents' house in Lawrence Weston, notably Wednesday evenings, her parents night for bingo. This worked well until one Wednesday when to our surprise and panic, they returned home early. We were in the back room in a state of undress; never before nor since have I dressed quite as quickly as I did that night.

There was one evening with Karen when we did go out. The local branches of the bank held a summer barbecue in a field on the outskirts of Bristol. I have to admit Karen and I were antisocial by not joining in the organised entertainment, instead we were planning entertainment of our own. We left the barbecue and crawled through the perimeter hedge to carry on in the way to which we had become so easily accustomed. We became quite dishevelled but felt, out of politeness, we should return to the barbecue party before it ended. This led to another comment from Derek the next morning when he exclaimed,

'You looked like you've been dragged through a hedge backwards!'

There was some truth in that.

Just before Christmas that year, we visited her aunt and family. She did not tell me that the purpose of the visit was to exchange presents. I was given a gift by her aunt and was expected to walk across the room and give her a kiss. To my shame I refused, despite much prodding by Karen; I was suffering an acute attack of embarrassment. The evening was also notable by the youngest in the family, a 12-year-old girl, Karen's cousin, flirting with me. They started young in that part of Bristol.

I was cavalier with the quality of my scooter riding. This would lead to quite a few mishaps with me falling off and injuring myself, thoroughly deserved. It should have been a different case when I had a girl riding pillion, but regretfully I didn't take my responsibilities seriously. Having caused Peggy serious injury, surely I would now be more careful. Not so. One night, taking Karen to a youth club dance at the church hall, I skidded on the gravel car park. We came off the bike, the windscreen shattered and the scooter buckled. As with my accident with Peggy, I was only scratched but Karen cut her arm and leg badly.

Mr Blacker from the bank (older than us so we always called him that, never by his first name, Tony) happened to be in the hall bar and very kindly took us both in his car to Southmead Hospital. Karen was in a really bad way and her injuries necessitated a return visit to hospital some days later. She lost a week at work. I called on her each lunchtime and usually found her in bed, but she was in no mood for any of that sort of thing.

Karen made me laugh with her wicked sense of humour. A current hit was 'The Ballad of Davy Crockett'. There was a joke doing the rounds about the resemblance of Davy Crockett's coolskin hat to a girls' pubic hair. Whenever the song was heard, or mentioned in conversation, Karen would laugh and, with a giggle, make a rude comment relating to pubic hair. She was like that.

She had many tales to relate, few were clean. Some I suspect were particularly unclean and would be shared only with her closest circle of girlfriends, not with me. After all, I was just an innocent bank clerk.

Later in our relationship I felt myself cooling towards her. One Wednesday, I was hoping for a quick getaway from her place to meet up with Mike and others for a late-night drink in town. So it was a pain my scooter chose that night to let me down -again - this time at her parents' house. I had no option other than to get the bus home, leaving my scooter on her front path. She walked with me to the bus stop. On the way I hummed, 'You've Lost that Lovin' Feeling', the current Righteous Brothers hit. A bit pointed, I suppose, and she immediately cottoned on to the hint.

'D'you mean that? Is that what yer really thinkin?'

She wasn't very well spoken. She continued,

'Chris, please, you can't leave me now!'

I tried to formulate a reply but didn't know how to answer. I just said,

'I don't know Karen, I am depressed about my scooter, we might be alright.'

Not really true.

Unkind of me to treat her like this as she had always been keen and good to me. I was not being fair, but I knew my feelings for her were on the wane. In spite of that, I couldn't break up with her while my scooter was still at her place.

It's not over yet. Karen was not going to let me go lightly: I was about to be tested.

The following Wednesday saw a change of direction. Karen, perhaps tired of our customary intimacy in the back room, invited me up to her bedroom. This caught me by surprise, I wasn't sure quite what to say or do. I followed her to the foot of the stairs. Up to this point I had done quite well with girls, but was still, just about, a virgin.

'Karen, I have no protection.'

'Chris, it don't matter, it really don't, I love you.'

She paused on the stairs before continuing,

'I don't want you to marry me if you gets me pregnant.'

Shock, horror, where is all this leading? Will we go all the way? Perhaps she should remind herself about the lyrics to the Shirelles hit, 'Will You Still Love Me Tomorrow?' before inviting me into her bed.

I did follow her into her bedroom and another session of moist activity followed, accompanied by heavy breathing. I went no further and it was clear this was a disappointment to her. Great self-control on my part as her fair skinned naked body was a delight to behold. She was a natural blonde. This was in the era of shotgun weddings and I was much too young for marriage. We dressed slowly and resumed our normal positions downstairs on the sofa. Nothing was said at the time but a few days later she referred to that night.

'Chris, you keep leadin' me on then don't go through with it. You're always lettin' me down.'

In a way she had a fair point but actually it was Karen who was leading me on.

We continued dating for a while after this, but eventually I decided enough was enough. I don't think I appreciated her as I should have done, she had been a cracking girlfriend. If I had been older and wiser the outcome might well have been very different. Would we meet again?

A little later I did see her again, at the Bristol Ice Rink. I was stumbling around the perimeter, no change there, when I felt a tap on my shoulder. It was Karen.

'Hi, great to see you again Karen! I would love to have a catch up, let's go for a drink when we finish here?'

'No thanks, Chris, really good of you to ask but I 'ave a new boyfriend now and I'm meetin' him later.'

Not long after this brief encounter, one of the girls in the office (thank you, Miss Jones) took pleasure in showing me a wedding photo in the Bristol Evening Post of a heavily pregnant Karen. I calculated that on our last proper date she must have been about two months pregnant, I hasten to add not by me. All along I believe her mission was to get married, perhaps to any boy she could persuade. A lucky escape for me. She was still a teenager; I wonder if the marriage lasted.

Shirehampton - a brief note

Shirehampton, always known locally as 'Shire', was originally developed due to being the lowest safe river crossing of the River Avon. It was then part of the parish of Westbury-on-Trym. The settlement has enjoyed a long history and outside the scope of this book, but one fact of interest that fascinates me is that, allegedly, the view from Penpole Point was mentioned in Jane Austen's 'Northanger Abbey'.

The village has many happy memories for me, and not just for being where I met Karen. I loved the time

I worked there. In the 1960s there was that feeling in the heart of the village, and perhaps is still there today, that 'everybody knows everybody'. It was a much quieter place then with a slower pace of life, with many characters.

Elderly Mr. White would be seen every day in the High Street, carrying his worn and well used outsized wicker shopping basket. Everybody knew and loved him.

Mr. Clark the greengrocer, something of a martinet, insisted to his staff - rightly - that bank notes in the till must all face the same way, as that is the manner in which he would be paying them into the bank. Saved me a job.

Mr. Cole the tobacconist, was a jolly soul and I was particularly taken with his striking blonde shop assistant, Gaynor. No date with her, but she did fix up a blind date for me with her friend and colleague, Sally, who I assumed would share the same good looks as Gaynor. I was well wrong there. I learnt in future to never assume.

12

ANOTHER SURPRISE

I was having an amazing time living in Bristol but then another surprise, indeed a shock, hit me. One morning I was called into the manager's office to be told I was being transferred to the Dursley branch of the bank. Having recovered earlier from the risk of having to move to Nailsea, in deepest Somerset, I was now facing another back of beyond destination to handle in Gloucestershire. As I was in receipt of lodging allowance, I was told I could not say no, and also that I would be expected to live in the town.

I complied with the move of branch, I had no choice, but on my first day at Dursley I told the manager I would not be moving accommodation. I would instead travel daily from Bristol, as the journey would take 'only' about an hour each way in my Austin A40. I didn't think my Lambretta, which I still owned, would be up to the job, and the idea of scootering up the A38 in the depths of winter did not appeal. The manager was not happy. He made his feelings clear,

'If you do this and are late for work just one day, your career, if not your job, will be on the line.'

I accepted the terms. And I was never late. Not once.

At Dursley, my responsibilities included liaising daily with our largest corporate customer, major exporters of farm machinery around the world. This role entailed checking shipping documents and the like, and chasing up reluctant payment from their purchasers. At last what I had learnt in my banking exams was to be put to good use. My days were long and tiring and I might have become quite dispirited had it not been for one extraordinary development.

A new typist arrived, quite attractive and taller than most of my previous girlfriends. I did not encourage her, I truly didn't, but for some reason she took a shine to me.

The office, as with most bank branches during that era, was divided into sections by high wooden partitions. Maria had her own cubicle. Twice a day I would call at her desk, first to deliver work, then later to collect the typed letters and such like. On seeing me, she would rise from her desk, fling her arms around my neck and give me a full-on passionate kiss. Quite an erotic experience at any time; during the working day this was something else, a real bonus.

Her soft moist lips were delicious and, to put it mildly, pure pleasure. I was more than happy with all this. She would not perform if the manager or a member of staff was in the vicinity; just as well. We never dated as such.

After a few months of this most agreeable activity, a new male cashier arrived at the branch and she transferred her allegiance to him. They married within weeks.

I was coping quite well as foreign trade clerk, but the cost of petrol, my bedsit and entertainment was becoming a financial strain. I had to find a part time job. Through a contact I found bar work in a notorious cider house in Bristol. My first and only stint working as a barman. I worked three nights a week at the starting pay of 4/6d per hour (22½p). No minimum wage to trouble employers. I must have impressed the landlady as this rate was later increased, dramatically, to 5/- (25p). The landlady had hard and fast rules.

'When you are not busy, you must stand with your arms to your side. I never want to see you with your hands in your pockets.'

The most popular tipple was known as dry cider.

'Never call it scrumpy', she demanded.

The sweeter, clear version of the drink was called, unsurprisingly, sweet cider. Even though this was a cider house, a barrel of Georges bitter was kept out of sight in the back room for the occasional beer drinker. When this was ordered, I was instructed to hold the glass well below the tap to create a bit of froth, this action being explained by the landlady,

'That's what the customer expects.'

Within twelve months of my move to Dursley I was transferred back to Bristol and able to give up the pub work. I enjoyed the experience, but was happy to move on.

I knew not what the future might hold for me but life was to get better, although not quite in the way I had imagined.

13

MARILYN

A good time girl (but in a nice way)

It was again my occupation that led me to meeting Marilyn. One of my rotating roles (we were moved regularly between local branches) was as a cashier at another sub office situated in the industrial zone of Avonmouth.

Marilyn worked for a major company there but I never knew what her job entailed. I didn't ask, and she didn't tell me. I spent too much time with my carnal thoughts when I should have been taking my time finding out more about her. She would call in once a week to cash her wages cheque. One of a crowd of female office workers, to me she was something special apart from being, to my eyes, drop dead gorgeous. Another lovely smiling lady blessed with an amazing crop of long blonde hair. We started dating.

There was a downside to Marilyn, for all her good looks, charm and personality. She was high maintenance in as much as she liked her drinks, either gin and orange or vodka and lime. Never would she ask for a less expensive drink, such as lager and lime or Babycham, more's the pity. Pub spirit measures being so small I could never escape with only buying her the one, I was still a modestly paid bank clerk. But she was good fun to be with, our relationship blossomed and was to become long term.

Marilyn was a passionate fan of the Four Tops, a popular soul and Motown American group from Detroit. I was also a fan of their music and in the car on a date we would sing lyrics from their hits and this somehow brought us closer. The Four Tops will make an appearance in a later chapter but in relation to another girl. Yes, they were a popular quartet, particularly with the ladies.

I always looked forward to my dates with Marilyn, particularly after a challenging day at work. *I ring her doorbell, she comes to the door, we kiss.*

One evening on one of our very early dates I was so happy I took her in my arms, gave her a squeeze and lifted her off her feet. The moment was perhaps spoiled by me involuntarily letting out a noisy fart. Not silent but thankfully not violent. Luckily for me, we were outside and not in her house, but her parents might still have heard my performance, it was quite a blaster. She gave me a funny look but no words of admonishment. Sorry, Marilyn.

Fairly early on I questioned her gently about any previous sexual encounters. Being three years younger than me I accepted she would still be a virgin. I was wrong. Quietly, she confided she lost her virginity to a young lad from Pill, the village I mentioned earlier, on the opposite bank of the river from her home in Shirehampton. She said she no longer sees him and anyway was not that fond of him. (She must have been *fairly* fond of him, I contemplated). This shocked and upset me. I was still something of an innocent. I was all for a healthy dose of heavy petting, but as I was still just about holding on the vestiges of being a virgin, I assumed the girls I knew would be the same.

Marilyn wanted to have fun and was keen on getting out, visiting pubs and clubs, so that is what we did. Some evenings she could be persuaded to spend at least part of the time at my bedsit to save me some of my hard-earned wages.

One such evening she asked if she could take a bath in the communal bathroom - a strange request, but I lent her my grubby towel and off she went. She returned 15 or 20 minutes later and seemed happy. Only later it dawned on me that perhaps she was hoping I would follow her into the bathroom and offer to 'scrub her back' or whatever. Or was there another reason for her taking a bath during our date? Perhaps there was, but either way I suspect that evening was, once again, one of my many missed opportunities.

A personal first was spending a weekend in a cottage in Wales with Marilyn: I had never been away with a girl before. I viewed her as a regular girlfriend but, by taking her away for a night, she might well have had every reason to believe I was looking upon her as something more.

The accommodation was quite basic with no running hot water, just a cold tap. For ablutions a kettle would be filled, put on the hob and once boiled, poured into an earthenware bowl and mixed with a jug of cold water. Marilyn told me this was quite a new concept for her. No hanky-panky on this trip, unfortunately, as we were staying with my parents in their rented holiday cottage.

She was keen to be involved in my life, something I did not appreciate fully. She took an interest in the trials and tribulations of my job and, as I admitted earlier, I regret not taking the same interest in her work.

I had explained to her that I was at the time a practising Catholic and, in another example of her wish to be part of my life, she asked if she could attend Christmas Midnight Mass with me. Which she did. In view of the dress code in the church in the 1960s, she was expected to cover her head. She found this quite bizarre and frankly I had to agree with her; the requirement has since been dropped.

But with nothing suitable to wear she popped down to Broadmead on Christmas Eve and bought herself a headscarf.

On Wednesday evenings her parents attended the same bingo hall Karen's parents frequented. So Wednesdays were again sofa time or, in Marilyn's case, fireside rug time, whereupon we would seek pleasure in our company, unless we were deep into one of our serious discussions.

This was the era of the BBC Wednesday Play, and one such production was the moving and heart rending 'Cathy Come Home', starring Carol White and directed by Ken Loach. We were mesmerised. That evening was one of our few platonic dates.

Some nights we would join up with another couple. On one such date, the four of us were highly charged even before we made a start on the beer and spirits. I had some trouble keeping up with Moses, who I had not previously met. He was Egyptian, but more than happy to imbibe. We drank some bonding beers and the girls had no difficulty downing their gins and vodkas. Glad it wasn't me driving. I was told by Moses' girlfriend that his driving was always very composed; this was not the case that night.

I was on the back seat, holding on to my girl, and suddenly felt very ill. Stop the van! Too late, as I spewed out over my trousers and unfortunately over Marilyn's dress. Embarrassing! Would I see her again? Yes, but I felt obliged to make a promise not to throw up again near her and certainly nowhere near her clothing. What with my earlier flatulence and now this, it was good of her to stick with me.

Then another foursome date. One fine evening Marilyn brought along a new companion by the name of Virginia, and I invited Mike to make up the four. Mike was keen to try out a pub at Keynsham, so merrily we made our way there with me driving my A40, which by now had become something of a passion wagon. We enjoyed a meal at the pub and a couple of drinks (actually several drinks for the girls).

We made our way home, stopping in a suitable layby to partake in the expected activities. I was enjoying a passionate kiss and a cuddle with Marilyn in the front of the car, and I presumed Mike would be doing the same with Virginia in the back. I was put off my stride a little, by plenty of huffing and puffing from the rear seats, combined with the sound of clothing being rustled. And I don't know what else. After a while we continued our return journey to Bristol. Mike was looking flushed. We dropped the girls at Marilyn's house and Mike and I returned to my place to reflect on the evening.

'Mike, everything ok with yours? You seemed to be getting some action, what did you encounter, throbbing thighs, heaving breasts, perhaps?'

'Not sure about that, but she was quite something. I really don't think Virginia is a very appropriate name for her.'

One night I realised Marilyn was planning to move our romance forward. We visited a cosy pub at Tormarton, where we both consumed too many drinks and my wallet was lightened as usual. I was unconcerned about driving as the breathalyser test was not introduced until the 1967 Road Traffic Act. We sat in the car before driving back to my bedsit for coffee and, with luck, a bit of action. Suddenly she whispered,

'You know, I do love you. Why haven't you told me how you feel?'

After a moment or two of hesitation I replied,

'I love you too, Marilyn.'

The words didn't sound right. I have never found it easy expressing my feelings and I wish I could have been more demonstrative, especially at times like this. Why did I have so much difficulty telling her how I felt? Was it because I wanted a girl, but not a long-term commitment? The result of my delayed response, and apparent lack of affection towards her, resulted in a less than satisfactory night to follow.

On another date she again asked me if I loved her.

'You say I am *lovely*, but do you *love* me?'

A pertinent question. I believe she did love me, and I feel sure we could have moved to a higher level. But I was young and taking life day by day.

In the 1960s, before the Biafran Civil War, international banks such as Barclays DCO and

Standard Bank of West Africa, were looking for UK staff to man their branches in Nigeria. The terms of service were most generous and I wanted to find out more. Martin introduced me to his uncle, a missionary in Nigeria, who was on a visit to the UK. Five of us, myself, Marilyn, Martin, his girlfriend Hazel and his uncle, met up for a drink and a quite serious chat. I gained much useful background information on the country.

It didn't occur to me until much later that Marilyn might well have been thinking I would be taking her with me, which would have meant going as a married couple, in view of the laws pertaining in Nigeria. Thinking of this now, and the weekend in Wales, was I misleading her? I fear I most certainly was, albeit inadvertently, and regret my conduct. My behaviour was again an example of me not being aware, and not realising, how my actions could impact on others. I am wiser now, but cannot put right what I might have said or done in my youth. I wish I could.

I was offered an interview with the Standard Bank and travelled to London for the interview, but with another girl, not Marilyn. Why not? What was I playing at? I cannot now remember the detail but perhaps Marilyn was unable to get the time off. A long day, catching the 7am train from Temple Meads and not arriving home until the early hours of the following morning. (Temple Meads was the only Bristol main line station for London, Bristol Parkway arriving later.) I was offered a job but, while I was prevaricating, the Biafran War broke out and all job offers were cancelled. Would there be another opportunity?

I kept in touch with Marilyn well after we had officially broken up. We were easy in our company and continued with casual dates until the end of the Sixties.

14

VARIETY IS THE SPICE OF LIFE

After my serious relationship with Marilyn I moved on, embarking on a footloose and carefree time of my life. I was again playing the field and looking forward to a break from the risk of commitment. Many of my encounters would be considered ridiculously innocent compared to today. Sex on a first or second date would be extremely rare among my circle of friends and colleagues, and the full works usually never happened, in spite of the so-called Swinging Sixties.

Miriam, not a girlfriend but a dominating supervisor at work, couldn't resist massaging my shoulders, not that they needed such treatment. She only worked on my shoulders, mind, we had an audience. This would occur, not in a quiet corner of the office, but whenever I walked into her processing room. Her girls there seemed quite unconcerned, perhaps seen it all before.

And there was another Mary, a minister's daughter, who believed a proper kiss might lead to pregnancy. Well, of course it could be argued every pregnancy starts invariably with a kiss, indeed the Hot Chocolate hit of 1982 was titled 'It Started with a Kiss', but clearly a kiss does not always lead to pregnancy. She was not convinced. I made little progress with her (well, actually no progress).

After a couple of years in my bedsit, I moved into a two bedroomed flat. This was not far from my previous pad so I was able to move myself with help from a couple of colleagues. I decided not to take the old sofa as by now it had been very well used. I promised my fellow removal men a drink before unpacking and, amongst the various boxes and general clutter, I offered them beers. For myself, I kept to the tipple I had recently discovered, Harvey's Bristol Cream sherry. I consumed half a bottle that day, and was very ill. I haven't given up on the occasional sherry but these days I keep to the dry variety. And in moderation.

After settling in, a couple of girls I knew vaguely from youth club days wandered into the flat. They were eating pots of yogurt, quite exotic to me, I had never heard of it. After a casual chat and an exchange of fleeting but pleasing mouth to mouth kisses, accompanied by a taste of yogurt (quite nice), they wandered out again. A trivial event, what was that all about? Sussing the joint? Checking perhaps if a hunk had moved in with me as a flatmate? Still a mystery.

Laura

Casual but nice

Soon after the move I met Laura, who was renting a similar flat up the road. With two flats between us there was no shortage of opportunities to be on our own. She could have used some time in the gym but was a kind-hearted soul. We shared an easy affinity so, as with Karen, we tended to stay in rather than go out. We got on well enough. I don't think there was any love between us, just good fun with new experiences. It was not to last but I relished the brief time we knew each other.

Iris

A country girl

While I was working at the main Bristol branch of the bank, Iris was the relief telephonist there. When not called upon to operate the switchboard, she had nothing else to occupy her time. The branch was very over-manned. My job at the time - a dividend processing clerk -also gave me plenty of free time. The bank was spread over four levels, including a dark basement which was used for storage of records. (I have just discovered, incidentally, that the bank closed recently and is now a posh hotel and restaurant with an up-market spa in this same basement.)

There were no work pressures on either of us, and certainly no sales targets to be met. Many a time I could be seen walking around the office with pen and paper in hand and an earnest look painted on my face. I was not actually working, of course, but I believed it looked convincing.

We enjoyed regular clandestine tête-à-têtes in the dark basement and would be unlucky to be spotted. Always nice to enjoy a kiss and a cuddle at work. She would place her hand on me to feel my arousal. We remained fully clothed though, as there was always the slight risk of being discovered.

We had only one proper date. She lived with her parents in a lonely cottage in Somerset along a winding farm track. After spending the evening in a country pub, I drove her home but stopped halfway along the track as she suspected her parents would be at home. They were not. We were enjoying ourselves exploring our bodies, she was exploring mine, I was exploring hers. Intriguingly, I noticed she had made liberal use of talcum powder down there prior to our date. I hazarded a guess as to why this might be, but then with a shock we saw through the steamed up rear window the headlamps of her parents' car coming towards us. Iris panicked, we straightened our clothing and drove on. All good fun.

Rosemary

Don't mess with the sisterhood

Prior to my stint at Dursley, I was allocated a two-week training course at the bank's Overseas Centre in the Pithay, Bristol to learn more about the financing of foreign trade.

The centre was staffed almost entirely by young girls, with a handful of older male staff filling management positions. I was in my element. Over the two weeks I arranged dates with three girls, all from different sections of the centre. Arrogantly I was enjoying myself and confident I was getting away with this multiple timing. It did not last long as I had not allowed for the sisterhood.

After a date with the third girl, I was taken aside by the lady in charge of the exchange control section. She was also responsible for all clerical staff and had heard about my exploits. She told me in no uncertain terms to lay off her girls.

I stayed with and settled on the third girl, Rosemary, or perhaps she settled on me. I remember her well for good reason. While we were dating, she gave me my first understanding of what tongues are for.

Alice

Sweet but not so innocent

I knew Alice initially from the Sunday night youth club. Later, she joined the main city branch of the bank where I was working. She was happy to spend evenings exploring pubs, and we became regulars at the Newman Hall bar where we would meet up with friends and colleagues. She was willing to pleasure me with intimacy in the car and I savoured those rousing moments. We experienced cherished times which would have been more comfortable in alternative surroundings but, whilst I tried my best, I could not persuade her to come back to my flat.

I did spend one evening at her place, to be shown, for the first time, a television programme in colour - 'Top of the Pops'. I was impressed. An innocent evening, though, chaperoned by her dad.

I never knew quite where I was with Alice, she was just *so* erratic. On one date she might be quite cold, but on the next would excite me with the behaviour of a nymphomaniac - and we would stop only scarcely short of a full consummation of our relationship. I went along with these changing moods, I had no option, but it would have been nice if she had always exhibited her compulsive desires.

> *'You tell me that you love me baby*
> *Then you say you don't*
> *You tell me that you'll come on over*
> *Then you say you won't*
> *You love me like a hurricane*
> *Then you start to freeze*
> *I'll give it to you straight right now*
> *Please don't tease'*

The night after one exceptionally torrid evening she quite suddenly dropped me, I later learned in favour of Jon, also originally from youth club. On reflection, perhaps she was disappointed with me for not responding fully to her advances on her 'hot' nights. Another squandered opportunity?

In spite of being discarded, I met up with her some while later at the hall and she agreed to me taking her home. All over me again. Yes, she was certainly erratic. Had she finished already with Jon? We continued with a few more dates, she would again lead me on into some very risky situations but eventually I was dumped for the second and final time. Then, surprisingly, perhaps to say 'no hard feelings', she gave me a gift, a green multi patterned tie. It was rather more attractive than it sounds. Why should I remember that? Strange how certain inconsequential events stay in the memory after so long.

Alice was brought up by her father, her mother having died shortly after giving birth to her. Not at all easy for a Dad to cope alone with a teenage daughter, particularly a girl like Alice. Some while after we had finished, I was returning to the bank after lunch when I spotted her on the steps by the front entrance, waiting for a lift. This was before the upper section of Corn Street, opposite the Corn Exchange, was pedestrianised. I said 'Hello' and returned to work, wondering why she should be leaving at 2pm. I discovered later she was on her way to have an abortion. I didn't think I had anything to be worried about personally, but out of interest I checked some dates in my diary.

Doris

Is it possible to see too much flesh?

I am grateful to my sister Sue for the introduction to this lively and sexy girl. Doris as a first name has fallen into disuse, but apparently is now making something of a comeback.

I was about to drive down to Devon to meet up with others for a camping holiday. Sue asked if I could first give her and Doris a lift to Swanage, where they were renting a caravan. I was offered the option of staying with them for a night to break the journey before proceeding on my way. I obliged, and the three of us set off for the south coast, Sue in the front seat, Doris in the back.

Nowadays, there is much concern about the dangers of using a mobile phone whilst driving. Seeing in the driver's mirror fleshy thighs and a miniscule skirt on a young girl is also quite a distraction. Doris radiated a jolly nature and was another lady with the habit of wearing her skirt, what there was of it, around her waist. She gave the impression of perhaps being up for anything. No way was I going to take anything for granted, but she was being very friendly…

We arrived in Swanage and unpacked. I had great hopes of getting personal and up close with Doris that night. I was still not well educated in foreplay and wondered what girls feel when touched down there. I knew where to find the spot that should respond to a sensitive touch, but that was about the extent of my knowledge.

Sue made a tactful visit into town for provisions and I took Doris to the caravan sofa. I used my knee to part her closed thighs. She reacted,

'Behave yourself!'

I had already experienced with Rosemary the touching of tongues, Doris now introduced me to an athletic version. Surely, then, she is not totally against my advances. I knew I had to be careful and not overstep the mark with my sister's friend, but she didn't resist my gentle encouragement and slowly spread her legs, just enough to let me make my approach.

I should clarify this was only a digital exercise, I was not using my manhood. I believed I could have taken proceedings so much further, yet again perhaps a missed opportunity, caused by my cautious nature and having nothing in my pocket apart from a very firm member.

15

NOT ALWAYS ABOUT GIRLS

My lifestyle was not always centred around girls, even if it might seem that way. Great fun was also to be shared with lads of a similar age. I was fortunate to enjoy a busy and rich social life during the 1960s, but while working at Avonmouth I had to find time to study for my Banking Diploma. This entailed night school for usually three evenings a week during the winter and spring terms. This ordeal took place at the Chamber of Commerce (now offices and flats) on Unity Street.

Apart from these evenings, a not inconsiderable amount of private study was also required. This took care of a good chunk of my evenings and weekends before going out on the town.

This social life with male company was based on visits to pubs, with evenings often ending at a chip shop or back home for coffee. These activities figured highly although were not exclusive pastimes.

During the week we attempted ice skating regularly. The journey to one such evening led to my first ever insurance claim. Mike and Bernie were with me; we were travelling along Cheltenham Road, approaching the Stokes Croft junction, when Mike distracted me by describing an experience with his girlfriend the previous night. I looked at him incredulously, oblivious to the fact that the traffic lights ahead had turned red. I ploughed into the car in front of me which in turn hit the car in front of that.

We plated ten-pin bowling at Kingswood and rather less frequently bingo (twice) at the old Savoy cinema in Shirehampton - the same bingo hall frequented by Karen's and Marilyn's parents.

Additionally, each winter I was lumbered with organising the inter-branch skittles tournament. I didn't exactly offer to do this, I was 'volunteered' and told it wouldn't do my career any harm. Perhaps not, but it didn't seem to do it much good either.

Weekends, apart from studying, would include shopping, trips to the Zetland Road launderette and occasionally, Mike, a keen Bristol City supporter, might take me to watch a match at Ashton Gate. Saturday nights would be either a party or dance -but only irregular success with the ladies.

For a short while I worked for a charity as an overnight volunteer on a Bristol telephone helpline. I chose to work on the Friday night shift and, as there would usually be two of us on duty, on quiet nights we would take turns to have a quick snooze. There were busy nights though and, on occasions, a telephone caller might then turn up at the office. This might lead to a visit to the Bristol Royal Infirmary or elsewhere. There would be no rest for either of us that night.

On the Saturday morning after my night shift, I might get an hour of sleep before my window cleaning round with Martin, one of his many money-making ideas. We were both invariably short of funds and the work brought in a bit of pocket money. Our normal charge was 8/6d (42½p) for a detached house; some were better value than others. One generous householder always rounded up our charge to 10/- (50p). Not surprisingly, we cleaned her windows more frequently than the others. One dear lady always offered us tea and biscuits, which was welcomed, very nice of her and all that and much appreciated. The downside was we fitted in fewer houses on those days and would barely cover our overheads - petrol for the car, purchase of cleaning equipment, a smoke both before and after each house and, at the end of the morning, a bag of chips covered with a portion of scrumps. Not a healthy addition to the chips but the scrumps were delicious, and free, and very welcome after a hard morning's work. A piece of fish would be added to our meal after a profitable day. And when the weather was warm, we might treat ourselves to an ice cream to add to our refreshment, but also to our costs.

All went well with this fledgling business until Martin suffered a nasty fall from his ladder (we were unaware of any health and safety regulations to be followed). We wrapped up the round soon after his accident.

I coped with working at the bank all week, then my Friday night helpline shift - resulting in a severe lack of sleep - then window cleaning on the Saturday morning, perhaps the laundrette and studying in the afternoon, followed by a party or dance on the Saturday night. Looking back, I am amazed I had the stamina.

On a free weekend, particularly if there was a bank holiday involved, we might be off to Wales, camping in and around the Roman gold mines at Pumpsaint. This site is now under the care of the National Trust and, whilst it is good for the area to be preserved for the nation, it is no longer possible to explore the caves and mines unaccompanied. That was a real fun activity, although no doubt highly dangerous.

Always on the lookout for new money-making ideas, it was Martin who suggested we tried visiting a casino. We found the Craywood Club on Queen's Road Triangle and, in some trepidation, presented ourselves at the club door. A pleasant receptionist pointed out, politely, that the law insisted we were members for 24 hours before we would be allowed to enter. We filled in our membership application forms, duly waited the requisite 24 hours and presented ourselves at the club the following evening. We were allowed in.

The only table we understood was the roulette wheel where we found ourselves seats amidst some of the hardened gamblers of the city. Our bets of half-a-crown a time (12½p) were exciting to us, no doubt tame compared with those around us. We were still poorly paid. As employees of a bank, under our terms of employment we were not allowed to gamble, so back at work we could not boast of any winnings. We did win some nights, my best visit being a profit of £2, but we were just as likely to lose. We broke even overall until one night our luck ran out. I was down £3 and Martin £4, a lot of money in the 1960s. That was our last visit, nevertheless one of life's experiences I do not regret.

Martin's next move was to buy a small sailing dinghy. This would be strapped, precariously, to the roof rack of his Triumph Herald, then off to Saltford where we would spend the evening on the river trying to sail the thing without falling into the water. 'Three Men in a Boat' we called ourselves as another wannabe sailor usually joined us.

These escapades clearly gave us a taste for water, literally in the case of some of our misadventures at Saltford. That summer, the three of us hired a motor cruiser for a week on the Norfolk Broads. We had no problem booking the boat, but I doubt if Blake's these days would hire to three irresponsible teenage lads. On our excursions we saw David Nixon on his boat, somewhat grander than our vessel, and walking along the seafront at Great Yarmouth was Joe Brown, but no sign of the Bruvvers. The holiday was not without minor calamities.

Day one was uneventful. Day two, we ran aground on mud and needed a tow to pull us into deeper water. Our third day was incident free but during day four I was at the helm and tried a quick turnaround. Unfortunately, the river was not wide enough at that point and we hit the bank, denting the bow. And on the last day, knowing we would not be reimbursed for fuel left in the tank, we ran it low. Too low as it turned out, and a tow to the boat yard was required. The boat company's manager was not best pleased, actually fuming mad, evidenced by the language he used. Still, we loved the holiday and even Martin's car breaking down on the way home, necessitating the three of us sleeping in the vehicle overnight, did not dampen our spirits.

That night in the car we tried to recall our best-loved jokes, even if none of us was particularly good at remembering or telling them. We did agree on one which more recently has done the rounds on the Internet. It concerns an elderly couple in a care home who had decided to get married. The widower didn't want to cause any embarrassment and courteously asked the widow what she thought about sex.

'I would like it infrequently,' she replied.

'Is that one word or two?' he ventured.

A year or two after the Norfolk Broads boating adventure I embarked on my first holiday abroad. Bernie and I booked a two-week package holiday to Lloret de Mar, flying from Luton Airport with Clarkson Holidays, now long gone, on a BAC 1-11 jet. 'Guantanamera' by the Sandpipers was playing in the aircraft as we taxied along the tarmac. Then lift off and we were on our way.

We arrived early evening on the Costa Brava, temperature 82° - Fahrenheit of course, Centigrade would not become familiar to us for many years. A coach transfer took us to our hotel where we dropped our cases and made haste to the town. We were greeted by an overpowering smell of suncream lotion, cheap perfume and greasy chips. Chips everywhere. Obviously, the intention of the holiday was to meet as many girls as possible. The reason this holiday is included in this chapter, 'Not Always about Girls', is for good reason.

On day three of the holiday Bernie became very ill, and I do mean *very* ill. He was out of action for several days. His bedsheets were not a pretty sight, being an interesting mixture of brown, yellow and magenta stains. His condition was perhaps not aided by our 'medicine cabinet' of gin, vodka and brandy. And the previous day is unlikely to have helped. We had explored the back streets of the town and endured a snack from the buffet table at a bar for locals. We were keen to see the real Lloret. Flies were having a feast on the food and yes, perhaps that might have been at least part of the cause of Bernie's ill health. I survived that incident in spite of my historic weak stomach. Later on, I was not to be so lucky.

Bernie reminded me recently of various embarrassing states into which I descended during the holiday. (You're a fine one to talk, Bernie). I have not forgotten the Rosamar night described below, but my memory is a blank as regards the other alleged incidents. I suppose the expression 'blind drunk' springs to mind, thereby perhaps my recollection of such events is understandably hazy.

We met several girls during the holiday but with little or no success. Every day was spent on the densely crowded beach, sunbathing and swimming, avoiding the raw sewage and rubber items floating in the sea as best we could.

'Ice cream, shocilar, licky licky', cried the beach vendors.

Plenty of late nights, bed before 2.00am and you were considered a lightweight. In the heaving bars and clubs, staff would leave the beer taps running between serving customers. It must have been so cheap to produce and not worth the effort to turn the taps off. The beer had a taste to match the price. Real ale it was not.

One night I overdid the 'champagne'- about 1/6d (7½p) a bottle - but an hour after bringing it all up, and ruining my much-loved suede shoes, we moved on to the Rosamar Hotel. There we stayed for the rest of the hours of darkness which ended with a platonic walk along the promenade with two young girls, Diane and Pat. A very warm night with many revellers lying in couples on the beach and being altogether 'friendly' until dawn. It's alright for some, we were very conscious of sorely missing out on the action.

Throwing up was a regular pastime in Spain for young people on holiday, all part of the package. In crowded night clubs it was not always possible to get to the loo in time. One young lady didn't make it. As she passed us, we watched her open her handbag which, luckily, was large enough to receive her evening set meal of chicken, peas, chips, something we were unable to recognise and a fair helping of a congealing dark yellow liquid. All good fun, happy days indeed. A memorable holiday.

One bank holiday weekend was spent with a large crowd of friends and colleagues on a narrowboat on the Grand Union Canal. Our stocks comprised a barrel of beer, a barrel of Somerset cider and boxes of basic foodstuffs. The weather was glorious, we were sunbathing on deck all weekend, and emptied both barrels. There was a mix of girls and boys on board but we slept separately - the weekend was to enjoy just the boating and alcohol, nothing more. Another one-off adventure.

Potholing was a girl-free activity, at least it was for our group. Cheddar is well known but we favoured

Burrington Coombe, a quieter gorge and just as challenging, where we found Goatchurch Cavern. This could be an exhilarating way to spend a Sunday afternoon. I was fairly adventurous in the caves, but not as adventurous, or foolish, as some.

I mentioned earlier there was no breathalyser test in those days, and we all travelled with jubilant abandon around Bristol and Somerset, initially by scooter and later by car. More than once I have referred to Somerset cider. A very early episode involved me on my Lambretta, and Bernard on his Matchless, spending an evening in the cider houses of Cheddar, drinking the 'proper stuff'. Somehow, I rode home. Bernard had to wake my parents as I was having difficulty managing the steps and my key to the front door. I lost two days at work over this, and have been extremely careful with the stuff ever since.

Alcohol was not our only vice. Drugs were around, we didn't use them, although we were all regular smokers. Ok, tobacco is a drug, but tobacco was big business in Bristol and it was considered both right and proper for us to support local industry.

We smoked in pubs, of course, in smoky cinemas, and during infrequent visits to restaurants when we had the money. Our dear friend Richard would smoke between courses, and sometimes *during* courses. No doubt unpleasant for fellow diners as his brand of choice was *Disque Bleu*.

Occasionally I would be tempted to a cigar. I really don't know why because I would become ill and throw up almost every time. I suppose being mixed with an excess of beer and probably chips would not have helped. Later I was to learn that cigar smoke should not be inhaled. Wish I had known that at the time.

The Corn Exchange was a popular venue for dances and jazz concerts. One Tuesday, I was given an alleged cure for a surfeit of beer. We were listening to a concert organised by the Chinese Jazz Club: that night the locally popular Blue Notes Jazz Band was playing. Jazz is not normally my thing but, on this occasion, I was absorbed with the atmosphere and overdid the ale. Again.

Derek, who was familiar with drinking to excess during his rugby days, suggested I would feel much better if I ran my wrists under a cold tap in the Gents, which I tried and yes, I felt a lot better. Not for long though, as I still threw up later that night. The building now forms part of St. Nicholas Market, so no more concerts or dances there.

On one of our early visits to the venue we had high hopes for a particular midweek function. This proved to be a disappointment. Chatting about what we might do instead, Bernard came up with an idea. He mentioned that acquaintances of his had summer jobs at Butlin's Holiday Camp, Minehead and suggested,

'How about riding down to meet up with them?'

It was about 10.30pm and I was on holiday so what the heck; I agreed. Quick visit home to pick up a few essentials and off we set, again Bernard on his Matchless and me on my Lambretta.

I suffered a major scare crossing Exmoor in the dark when a deer leapt out in front of me. I wobbled to a very shaky stop, somehow managing not to fall on the road. I was dazed by this frightening incident and it took me a few minutes to recover, by which time Bernard had returned to see what had happened to me. No bones broken and we continued on our journey.

With an absence of further mishaps, we arrived at Butlin's in the early hours. Bernard had been told the location of a hole in the fence and we eventually found the right chalet. A popular light-hearted observation then, and perhaps even today, was,

'The fence is to keep campers in, not to keep trespassers out.'

Surely there can be no truth in this statement but it's a nice story, and the quip was included in a BBC 'Two Ronnies' sketch in the 1970s.

No worries about being woken up with 'Good Morning Campers', as the speakers had been vandalised. We stayed a second day at the camp before continuing our travels, camping the next night in a hay barn close to Tarr Steps on Exmoor. We rose early to avoid the farmer and continued our journey, stopping for breakfast at an all-night cafe. As we arrived, '24 Hours from Tulsa' by Gene Pitney was playing on the juke box. We enjoyed a hearty breakfast and, replenished, headed home to Bristol.

One weekend a while later we heard about a party at Avonmouth. Three of us gate-crashed what was a very boring party with few eligible girls in attendance. We had taken plenty of beer in the form of Courage Jackpot four-pint cans and, with drinks already at the party, we enjoyed a merry evening.

The time came to drive back along the Portway to Bristol, and we agreed it might be fun - we were young - to try a car share. We were using my car, so I sat in the driver's seat operating the pedals. The passenger next to me operated the gear stick and the third leant over my shoulder to operate the steering wheel. We made it home.

That's a real car share; eat your heart out Peter Kay.

16

- BUT IT USUALLY WAS

Girls could be so different in the manner of their embrace. One girl might prefer to keep daylight between us, whereas another would press her body into mine. I quite liked that and would reciprocate. Some girls were undoubtedly keener than others, or less inhibited. More than once I would make a note in my occasional diary, along the lines of 'cinema tonight, film lousy but I had a great time.' Or, depressingly, some notes would read 'film great, lousy night.'

I forget the name of the girl with the allegedly aggressive father, probably because I lasted only one or two dates with her. Before I called at her house for our first date, she warned,

'If Dad's car is on the drive, don't come in. Mum's ok, you don't want to meet him.'

I was grateful for the warning. I never did meet her dad but the girl had conjured up in my mind quite an image. I played it safe.

Our group kept in touch with several of the girls from our youth club days. Often, we really were just good friends and might, as a crowd, take a Sunday trip to the Somerset coast for a walk, and rarely did any particularly serious relationships develop. Happy commitment-free days. I did find myself attracted to one girl, Christine. I cherished a couple of dates with her, including a wonderful day on the Downs. An idyllic time. This was all fairly platonic but no less enjoyable for that. Bernie also dated Christine, I'm not sure if he was before or after me. I asked him recently to remind me how he got on,

'Ok, but platonic.'

Seems she was into platonic dates. Sadly, I was out of luck with her as a smooth guy by the name of John swept her off her feet. He had quite a reputation with the ladies and seemed able to charm any girl. I bet *he* proceeded beyond the platonic date. Not that I'm bitter or anything…

An early brief contact was with Jane, an amazing girl with auburn hair who could best be described as rather posh. I was obsessed, innocently I hasten to add, I was not stalking her, honest. One Sunday night after a church hall dance, she let me walk her home to an elegant and imposing house in a smart part of Henleaze. My time with her was to be very short lived. I was allowed a fleeting kiss and tried for a date.

She said no. She gave no reason, just a simple but polite 'No thank you'. A disappointment as she was quite a stunner. Was I not in her league? Probably she could have chosen any boy she wanted.

Another of my many failures was Sheila, a pleasant Irish girl. I contrived for my scooter to 'break down' outside the nursing home where she had a Saturday morning job. I waited for her to finish her shift. The plan worked: I caught her as she came out of the home and started to chat her up. She claimed to be in a rush as she was hoping to call on a girlfriend. I said,

'Is she expecting you?'

Unfortunately, she didn't hear the word 'you' and assumed I was being offensive. I had developed the trace of a Bristol accent since moving up from Wiltshire, and with the combination of the two intonations I guess my speech lacked some clarity.

This was not a very good start with Sheila, nevertheless she agreed to a date at the Odeon, Broadmead to see the recently released 'The Sound of Music'. I called round at the arranged time. She greeted me with a rebuff,

'Sorry, I've changed my mind.'

She gave no reason; I watched the film on my own.

I met Sylvia at the Top Rank Ballroom one Saturday night and, surprisingly, made a date with her for the following week. I say surprisingly because I rarely had success at this venue. Or at any dance hall, for that matter. Others were luckier, as evidenced by a dance at the Victoria Rooms, with Bernard. He met Helen there, they became serious, and later married. No luck for me with my girl that night, par for the course.

Anyway, I had this date with Sylvia, a few drinks in the pub which was ok. She was wearing a CND badge; the organisation had a high profile at the time. She gave me not one, but three photos of herself, proudly displaying her badge, on this our first date. This was a surprise as photographs were rare, not like the hundreds taken today with the benefit of digital cameras and mobile phones.

Sylvia was a very committed girl with strong principles, and I admired her for sharing her beliefs with me, as she would not have known whether or not I shared her views. She asked if I would be prepared to join her on the next Aldermaston march. I declined, really for not knowing how it would all pan out rather than a lack of support for her. We drifted apart. I am glad she gave me those photos. I regret I was not given more of girls I knew. I know I am stating the obvious, but special memories are captured and remembered this way. The few I did possess were treasured.

I played a particular prank on certain girls if we were in a public place, and if the girl was wearing a dress with a rear zip. Tenderly I would place a hand on the back of her neck and run a fingernail down the outside of the zip. My victim would be horrified, as this action on my part gave the impression of being undressed. Most girls would be fine with this - once they realised they were not having their dress removed in public. On one such occasion I tried this on with a girl I did not know well. Before the girl had cottoned on to what was happening (or actually not happening), most unwisely I said,

'I'm imagining you with no clothes on, and I like what I see!'

This resulted in a questioning frown on the girl's face, followed a moment later with a heated exclamation,

'How rude!'

Ah, it's the little things that bring such pleasure. I was lucky to get away without a slap that night but I did lose the girl with my silly comment. I was told a few times I could be a right bugger with some of my tiresome ways.

My zip trick wouldn't work with Pauline because she never wore a dress, always jeans and a blouse. I met her at the garage round the corner from my flat where I took my cherished A40 when it was in need of tender loving care. She was the cashier there and immediately I was attracted to her. I asked her out, she accepted and after the routine drinks at a pub we returned to her flat at Fishponds for coffee and to get acquainted. We didn't get to the coffee. With no time lost we were on her bed, but fully dressed, and I was getting just a tad worked up. In the excitement I had a little accident. Oh dear. Perhaps I am divulging too much personal information here but I did say at the outset I would tell it as it was, no holding back.

Whilst on the subject of holding back, premature ejaculation can be a problem for the young, just as erectile dysfunction often affects the elderly. Seems if it's not one thing that gets you it's the other. And there is something else that illustrates the difference between a young lad and an old man. When at school I could point Percy at the porcelain and have competitions with other boys as to who could aim the highest. Today it is more a question of keeping my shoes dry.

Before leaving Pauline to make my way home, I asked for another date. This time she declined, perhaps she already had a boyfriend or perhaps simply didn't fancy me that much. Never mind, can't win them all.

There was one specific occasion I remember well, but again cannot recall the girl's name. We were lying half dressed, but quite innocently, between the sheets. Blankets and sheets then, duvets, or continental quilts as they were originally known, did not gain popularity until the early 1970s. We had no specific plans apart from cuddling up close. Between those sheets she whispered,

'Chris, will you let me see it, you know, your thingy?'

I recollect the saying, 'I'll show you mine…' but I said nothing and obligingly lifted the sheet, exposing myself to let her have a peep. Ah, such innocent days. Like most men I like to think I am adequately blessed in that region. Years earlier, I had come second in a competition behind the school bike sheds, so I was keen to hear what she thought, and was looking forward to hearing her comments. The girl said nothing, she just smiled. Was that a good thing? Or not?

17

1966 AND ALL THAT

Most men when asked what they know about 1966 will reply,

'The year England won the World Cup, England 4, West Germany 2.'

Here we are, 50 plus years later, still living the dream. I was unable to watch the match as I was driving home from Liverpool, having attended my brother's wedding the previous day. A long journey, with the motorway network in its infancy. I arrived back in Bristol and, thanks to the match going into extra time, just made it to hear Kenneth Wolstenholme exclaim,

'They think it's all over…it is now!'

After the match Mike, myself and Bernie drove to the New Forest for a two-week camping holiday. My parents had a tent, only used once, so we took it along. We found a suitable spot in a delightful glade beside a forest stream. We unpacked the tent. I had never actually seen it in use before and was shocked when Mike exclaimed,

'It's a *ridge* tent!'

We were expecting a modern frame tent. I was not popular and it was pointed out, fairly politely in the circumstances, that I should have checked this beforehand. Too late to change our plans, we had to make do.

The tent was erected, a few beers consumed at the local pub, then time to crash. Bernie was always first to get his head down and he volunteered to sleep at the back of the tent, curled around the end support pole. Mike christened him 'The Banana.' During the first night a storm broke. We were woken to find ourselves marooned by the said forest stream, now an over-flowing torrent. We packed our soaked bags, tent and the rest of our paraphernalia and drove off in search of somewhere dry.

We came across a disused railway station with a waiting room. Perfect! The door had been sealed, not a problem for us as the window was not locked. We climbed in and were about to settle down for the night on the bare floor… but first I had a concern. I spoke to the others,

'If we can get in so easily, others can and they might not be too friendly.'

The point was taken and we rested the iron fireplace grate against the window to warn of anyone else who might be looking for free and dry lodgings. We slept surprisingly well that night.

Next day we found a relatively dry spot, well away from the stream, and set up camp once more. Now the holiday could start!

The railway station, incidentally, has since been converted into a tea room and tourist information centre.

First port of call following the delayed start to our holiday was the Queen's Head pub at Burley. We were in luck, meeting up with a group of girls on a coach holiday from Cheshire. Good for a kiss and a cuddle, but we didn't see them again. No worries, we were looking forward to Bournemouth.

We were not camping on a recognised site, so no fees to pay. The downside was an absence of facilities, notably toilet facilities. Plenty of bushes for a pee, uncomfortable for anything else. Consequently, each day started with a trip to Boscombe public toilets, crudely referred to by us as the Boscombe Crapper. A welcome and necessary visit. Once this was taken care of, we would make haste for the sea.

Our days, lazy days, were spent on Boscombe beach, just to the east of Bournemouth, swimming and sunbathing - parking was easier there compared to Bournemouth. Bernie had brought along a large brass telescope which was used to good effect to review the talent on the beach. Perhaps surprisingly, we were never accosted about our 'Peeping Tom' activities.

At the end of the day it was back to the tent to cook cauldrons of potatoes to line our stomachs for the beers we planned to consume later. Evenings consisted of visiting local hostelries prior to either the Pavilion dance hall, or a discotheque such as Le Kilt or Samantha's. These visits had one purpose in mind. Some nights we might be lucky, some not so. The one constant theme throughout the fortnight was an abundance of Swedish, Dutch and French female students.

Whilst this gave a continental flavour to the holiday and some of the girls were real crackers, we were faced with the language problem and conversation could be an issue. The girls I spoke to generally had a good command of English, but Mike was not so lucky. In exasperation, he once called out at a Pavilion dance,

Is anybody here English?'

Fairly early on, we met a group of Dutch girls and spent a day or two with them. They were not very responsive, nor to be frank were they particularly easy on the eye. But we were on holiday when standards on both sides of the gender divide tend to be flexible, and we were looking for a bit of action, regardless. The Dutch girls became history when we teamed up with Swedish students we met at Samantha's. They were much more responsive and spoke very good English, yet were puzzled by the odd word. Their hostel was in the centre of town.

'That's handy', I commented.

'What does "handy" mean?', one asked.

We spent pleasurable time with them in the car between pub stops. Our athletic activities caused the car to become severely steamed up with rivulets of moisture running down the insides of the windows. Mike commented,

'This could be the first time a car rusts from the inside.'

We invited the girls for a drink at The White Hart, just outside Burley, where Adge Cutler and the Wurzels were playing. Not the first time I would encounter this West Country band. Later that year on 2nd November they recorded their first album, 'Live at the Royal Oak'.

This was the Royal Oak, Nailsea and I was there on that memorable and special night. Regrettably, we were not able to squeeze ourselves into the already packed upstairs room where the recording was taking place, but we were able to listen to the enthusiasm of the proceedings from the ground floor bar. Sadly, Adge was killed in a road accident in 1974 at the age of 42 years.

In his memory, a bronze statue has been erected outside the Royal Oak. Go see it. It would be good if you were able to enjoy a pint of his favourite tipple while there, except you will not have the pleasure. Recently I visited the pub and downed a pint; enjoyable, but it was not the experience I had been expecting. The pub has been taken over by Greene King, and on my visit, I could find no reference to Adge inside the pub - a criminal omission. Equally bad, the pub was selling cider from elsewhere, not genuine local Somerset cider.

I digress. Returning to the Swedish girls: after the White Hart we took them to our tent. Swedish girls had a certain reputation, and no doubt still do. They were quite uninhibited but the evening did not progress beyond the undoing of belts, bra straps and the like. I am speaking for myself here, I cannot comment on what Mike and Bernie might have been getting up to that night. I formed quite an attraction to my girl, Bodil, and we remained pen pals for a couple of years. We had every intention of meeting up again in the UK or Sweden but the hoped-for reunion never materialised.

Towards the end of the fortnight we were joined by one of Mike's university friends - Stewart - and the four of us spent a day in Swanage, parking easily in the High Street. We enjoyed a swim, a few beers and a tasty fish and chip supper. On return to the car we were dismayed to be faced with a £3 parking ticket.

By now, in Bristol, restricted parking on roads had been annotated with double yellow lines. This practice had not yet reached Swanage where, unbeknown to us, we should have looked out for 'No Parking' signs. We were in my car and generously the lads agreed to split the fine four ways. I am still waiting for Stewart's contribution.

A memorable holiday but an issue in the back of my mind was causing me concern. In Bristol, I was dating two girls and was keen on them both. I had to make a decision.

18

LILY - PART 1

In the beginning

In the 1960s, my relationships didn't get more serious than with Lily, albeit not immediately. A lovely girl, a full head of dark hair, amenable, quite short but well endowed. It was not love at first sight although, in time, we were to become very close, intense and passionate. This encounter with Lily was not through the bank this time, but as a result of my 21st birthday party held at my parents' Nailsea farmhouse a few weeks before the 1966 World Cup. Mum and Dad had recently sold up in Redland and moved to the country: the farmhouse served as an ideal location for my celebrations.

As the day of the party approached, there was a serious risk there might be a shortage of girls. I approached Martin. His girlfriend, Hazel, worked at a children's nursery at Portishead, so could he get his girl to bring along some of her nursing colleagues? He did ask, she agreed and, thanks to fate, Lily was in the group. I made little impression on her that night, and instead started a short flirtation with the rather vivacious Edwina, who was in the same nursing crowd.

During the next week I had a couple of dates with Edwina but couldn't get Lily out of my mind, I was day dreaming about her and having difficulty concentrating on my job. I gently called it a day with Edwina and fixed up a date with Lily.

We were to be together for two emotional and sometimes tumultuous years, and she became the light of my life, but we were apart for one summer when she took a nursery nurse role at Butlin's, Pwllheli. This was to be followed by a new job in her home town of Peterborough. I will explain shortly why, instead of Peterborough, she returned to Bristol and her job at Portishead after her summer job. I remember the time well.

I continued to maintain limited contact with Marilyn while dating Lily. These were the two girls I referred to in my previous chapter. I was very keen on both but had arguments with each of them, or at least minor disagreements. These could lead to long and deep discussions. Lily was always quietly spoken and would never raise her voice. Marilyn was more outward, although not unduly so. I had heart searchings with myself over both girls.

I was in a quandary and knew I had to make a choice. One lunchtime, I asked an older male colleague at work for advice. He was something of a father figure. I invited him for a drink at Molly's Bar, just round the corner from the office. Once we were settled with our halves of Georges bitter and sandwiches, I put my dilemma to him. He gave his advice.

'If you can't decide between them, neither can be right.'

I didn't agree with him at the time and felt he was being unhelpful. Later, I realised his comments - up to a point - did make some sense and shortly after our chat, I believed I was dearly in love with Lily but only extremely fond of Marilyn. Therefore it can only be Lily. What might have happened if I had decided on Marilyn, assuming she agreed to stay with me? Such decisions define our destiny.

In the early days of our courtship (does anyone still refer to 'courtships'?), a typical date would begin with me waiting in my car across the road from her dormitory at the Portishead nurses' home. From the window she watches for my arrival. She joins me and the evening commences with a drink in a pub in Portishead or Clevedon - pint for me, Babycham for Lily - before making our way to the coast road to find our special layby. We move into the back seat for a cuddle and sometimes more. On an early date I caressed her generous breasts for the first time. I recollect her words to me,

'I have never let a boy do that to me before.'
Lily was one of the worlds' innocents.

We spent time in the company of Martin and Hazel. Over drinks one evening one of us, no doubt Martin or myself, the girls would not be that forward, suggested a weekend for the four of us in Bournemouth. Martin and Hazel were an established couple, but this was quite an adventurous suggestion for Lily and myself, being in the early days of our romance. Still, the trip was agreed and off we set.

First stop on our arrival was a visit to Bournemouth Pier Theatre to buy tickets for 'Rattle of a Simple Man' starring Hugh Lloyd. We then duly booked into a B&B in Boscombe, 12/6d (62½p) per person per night. It didn't take long for the suspicious landlady to sum up the situation and gave us two twin bedrooms - one for the girls and one for the boys. There was a bit of scuttling along the dark corridor and opening and closing of doors but, in the words of the landlady, there was no opportunity for any 'funny business.'

I was introduced to Lily's parents in Peterborough. On the date of my first visit there we were watching television when news broke of the Aberfan disaster in October 1966. Another unforgettable visit was in November 1967 when we watched Harold Wilson announce sterling was to be devalued - his 'pound in your pocket' speech.

It was on this visit that my previously faithful A40 broke down barely half way back to Bristol. I had no option but to arrange to abandon the car at a local garage and for us to hitchhike the rest of the journey. We were picked up by a very amenable couple who insisted on taking us all the way home. Thanks to them, and thanks to you, Martin, for driving me to the garage to collect the car a few days later. Repair bill £8/3/6d (£8.17½p) for labour and a new head gasket.

I was devastated when, just under a year into our time together, Lily moved to Butlin's for her planned summer job. I had fallen in love with her, ripples of pain ran through my heart when she confirmed she had not changed her plans and would be leaving me. Now for that second reference to the 'Four Tops' I mentioned in the Marilyn chapter. As I was driving Lily to Temple Meads, she gave me for my birthday an LP by the group, knowing I was keen on their music. That, combined with our imminent separation, brought a lump in my throat and tears to my eyes. It was raining in my heart, to use the title of a Buddy Holly hit from 1958.

I continued as best I could without her and had a few casual dates with other girls, including Marilyn, after Lily left. But my heart was not in other dates, I was far from happy. I discussed my predicament with my old school mate David. We decided to spend a couple of lazy days in Wales, visiting Pumpsaint and

Aberystwyth, sleeping in his van, and then drive to Pwllheli. He drove up from Trowbridge, picked me up and off we set for Wales. I wrote to Lily to let her know I was coming to see her.

On arrival at Pwllheli two days later, I called her from a phone box outside the holiday camp, *(insert four pennies; press button A)*. She agreed to meet me at the end of her shift by the main entrance to the site. I waited, stomach churning, heart racing and then I saw her, walking slowly down the drive. We met, I moved to kiss her on her mouth but she deflected me to her cheek. Words would not come easily. After a few moments I stuttered,

'Lily! I have missed you so much! I am incredibly happy to see you again. You must come back to Bristol, you really must!'

I continued in this vein for some time and struggled to maintain my composure. She said she would think about my plea but her new job in Peterborough was ready and waiting for her. I wondered what was going through her mind at that moment - perhaps how to let me down gently?

Happily, my efforts paid off as she wrote to me shortly afterwards to confirm she had changed her plans and was being given back her old job at Portishead. We were soon to be reunited. The love of my life was coming home.

19

LILY - PART 2

'Thank you for the days'

On 20 August 1967 I collected Lily from Temple Meads station. An emotional reunion, I was in Paradise. We continued our life together.

A week or two after her welcome return, we spent an unforgettable Saturday afternoon at Cheddar Gorge. We walked up Jacob's Ladder, a long flight of steep steps to a high point above the gorge, and sat on the grass. We looked at each other, we smiled and I put my arm around her. We lay back, we kissed. We were alone and I treasured the moment. I became aroused but this was early in our renewed courtship and Lily still appeared to be innocent and inexperienced, apparently not having been led astray by the over - sexed Redcoats at Butlin's.

By now I was established in my flat in Roslyn Road, Redland. The night after our day in Cheddar we spent at the flat, we did not sleep. We enjoyed prolonged and passionate embraces, and lingering kisses, some with our eyes open. We might part yet still hold our gaze, not smiling, just looking at each other, in silence.

I was in love - but was she? I proposed; no reply came. We then talked about everything and nothing until, with much surprise, we realised it was 6.00am. We walked slowly through Redland and down to Cheltenham Road Arches; I remember the area was surrounded by noisy pigeons. We meandered our way back to the flat, including a stroll along Lovers Walk. Then a drive to Portishead as Lily was on duty that morning. To date the most joyful weekend of my life? I was in Heaven and on a high.

I was happy where I lived, happy in my job and I had a girl who I believed loved me - although she had not accepted my proposal. I'd never had it so good, or so I believed. Will this blissful state of affairs last for ever?

We were now spending all our free time with each other. At weekends, if Lily was not on duty, we might take a drive into the countryside or perhaps visit Weston-Super-Mare. On our journey back to Portishead or Bristol we would sometimes stop at Clevedon to watch the celebrated sunset over the pier, standing hand in hand. A romantic spot for a couple in love.

One Saturday, we planned a day trip to Bournemouth. Too cold for swimming, instead we chose a romantic walk along the beach and promenade; quite delightful. We followed this with a drive to the New Forest for an evening meal. By now it was getting late so we found a layby and slept in the car. I cannot recall how we managed for toilet facilities, but it was a deserted layby.

Sometime later, I felt the time approaching when we would progress to sexual activity. One night in my flat I felt to be the right time but was worried I had no protection. I was under the influence of the Catholic church who have never allowed any form of 'mechanical' contraception. Nevertheless, a most memorable night was to follow.

It should have been a tight squeeze, sharing a single bed, but we were happy and comfortable to be in such close proximity to each other. We were both of a slender build which helped. There she lay, wearing her pink nightdress with the pattern of tiny roses. And underneath? No panties. This surprised me, as I had assumed she would have kept them on. I was sure she was still a virgin. I lingered, savouring the moment. I moved nearer, much nearer, closer…

'What are you doing?', she exclaimed, in a voice louder than normal for her.

What sort of question is that, I thought? Surely at her age she knows the facts of life? Perhaps not. I muttered, lamely, the first words that came into my head,

'Nothing much.'

Such a weak reply! I couldn't think of the right words to say, I wasn't prepared to be quizzed on my advances. That was a really poor response to her quite justified question, but then, considering how that night actually progressed, the event was indeed, 'nothing much'.

I was careful not to take advantage of her innocence during this experience. It would be wrong to take her down a path that might make her uncomfortable or even distressed. It is possible I could have proceeded further that night with her acquiescence as, on a similar occasion shortly afterwards, I gained the vague impression the initiative was being taken by her. I might have been mistaken and more likely this was just wishful thinking on my part. I am grateful I did not make excessive advances on her that night, bearing in mind my later shameful treatment of her. More on that later.

Soon after that night, I proposed to Lily a second time, standing with her in the centre of Clifton Suspension Bridge. A more romantic spot would be hard to find in Bristol, or anywhere else for that matter. She accepted my proposal.

We celebrated with a camping trip to Wales, pitching the tent adjacent to the Roman gold mines I knew from earlier visits. This trip was again with Martin and Hazel, and all good and mostly innocent fun was to be enjoyed. We shared a tent, so no privacy for the ladies and no facilities such as a toilet block, but there were several trees and plenty of bushes. I have to say the girls were very game to go along with this primitive form of camping.

We used an old primus stove to heat up water for hot drinks and basic meals. Very basic meals. For anything substantial it was off to the pub in the village for drinks, food and welcome use of their questionable toilets.

One fine day we drove to the coast and had great fun scrambling over the rocky shoreline, Martin still wearing his tie. I have a photo to prove to disbelievers that this was irrefutably the case. He has always maintained a certain standard of dress although now, in retirement, he has been known to dispense with the tie.

During our next visit to Peterborough we told her parents of our intentions. Did I formally ask for her father's permission? I do not recollect doing so as such. I did state that, in line with Catholic doctrine, we would be married in a Catholic church, and any children would be brought up in the faith. This did not go down too well, I suspected because her father was a warden at their Methodist church.

On our occasional weekend visits to Lily's parents I was expected to accompany the family to their church for Sunday Service. This I was happy to do, a new experience for me and, anyway, I had earlier taken Lily to Mass. I was surprised how noisy the Methodist congregation was, both before and after the service, very different to my church.

Nothing specific was said by her parents at the time about the Catholic Church teaching, but Lily told me that on a later occasion her father spoke privately to her,

'If the Catholic church think they can impose that on you, they can take a running jump.'

His exact words, apparently.

Back in Bristol, our love was not all plain sailing, nothing serious to start with, just little hiccups. I can give one example. Earlier, I mentioned that each winter I organised a skittles tournament between the Bristol branches of the bank, with matches played at various pubs in and around the city. I took Lily to some of these evenings. On one of these social events we had another of our quiet arguments, I forget now what it was all about. She decided to stay in the car, in a huff, for the duration of the skittles match. This was much to my acute embarrassment as my colleagues were well aware of the situation.

On some dates, she would be even quieter than her usual self without telling me what was troubling her. Clearly there would be something on her mind and this did not always tally with her cycle. Mysteries of the fairer sex.

One weekend I suggested a weekend camping trip to Beer, next to Seaton on the south Devon coast. This time just Lily and myself. No pre-planning, we chucked into the car a couple of sleeping bags, the tent from the New Forest lads holiday and a few essentials. Off we drove. I have no idea where or what we ate, but I do remember we both suffered serious sunburn from too many hours lying on the sun-trapped beach. Back on the campsite, I captured a delightful photo of Lily sitting outside the tent admiring the glorious coastal view. A perfect weekend - in spite of the sunburn.

I should now be lavishing all my affection, love and unbridled attention on Lily but something was wrong. Sadly, my ensuing behaviour left a lot to be desired. Remember it was me who persuaded her to return from Butlin's and share her life with me.

During my active dating years, I had my suspicions I was sometimes being two timed by girlfriends. I never had any such suspicions with Lily and profoundly regret I was not so faithful towards her. When she was working an evening shift, I might be tempted to seek my pleasures elsewhere. I am still full of remorse over my behaviour at a particular party I held at my Redland flat. It pains me to put my behaviour into words, but I must. It is a confession of my guilt.

Lily was going to be late arriving at the party, owing to her shift. While waiting for her to arrive, I started chatting up a girl I had always fancied - lovely Cindy from the bank typing pool. She had earlier given me hope I might be in with a chance when she gave me a gift, an ashtray she had bought on a holiday in Spain. It shows my immaturity that I should even dream about making approaches towards Cindy, or any other girl for that matter, as I was ostensibly happily engaged to Lily. Quietly we crept upstairs to a spare bedroom for cuddles and some very personal exercises, the girl being very compliant to my advances. During proceedings, she whispered,

'You must think me awful!'

'No, certainly not, Cindy,' I lied.

A very willing girl was encouraging me and thoughtlessly I was enjoying myself. We didn't stay long as I was hosting the party and hadn't forgotten Lily was due to arrive. We gingerly walked down the stairs to mingle unobtrusively into the party, but I was shocked to come face to face with Lily at the bottom of the stairs, her shift having finished early. She was trembling and in tears, being comforted by a male guest at the party. Someone had implied to her where I was and what I was likely to be doing.

Shortly after this fateful party, I bought her a scooter, a Vespa 125cc, to reduce her reliance on the bus service and make it easier for her to travel between Portishead and Bristol. On reflection, I suspect this purchase was to make life easier for me rather than for her.

Within weeks of buying the scooter, I hinted in a roundabout way that I was not sure of our future.

She broke down in tears. But we did sleep together that night. Sleep, that is, nothing more.

This was not right. My feelings for her were undeniably cooling and I knew I must do something about it. One stormy night at my flat I admitted it was not working out for me and we must split up. I started to drive her back to Portishead, but the storm worsened and the car died at Abbot's Leigh, just outside Bristol. This was not good timing and most unfortunate, creating a very uncomfortable situation for us both.

Luckily, we were next to a phone box - no mobile phone of course. I phoned Bernard who was happy to drive out on a rescue mission. He returned us to my flat where, silently, we spent the rest of the night. The date - 10th July 1968 - the night of the Big Storm, which caused much destruction including Pensford Bridge being washed away. In the morning, weather still dreadful, Lily caught an early bus to Portishead and a return to work.

I had left it too late before facing up to the increasing certainty we would part. Wedding plans were proceeding apace and Lily's mother had bought the material to make her dress. When her parents were told of our split, her Dad made an apposite comment,

'Better to get divorced before the wedding rather than after.'

I wish I could make amends for my inexcusable treatment of her. I cannot undo the hurt I caused, but could she ever find it in her heart to forgive me? I fear that is surely too much to ask.

Her comforter at that party, by the way? Another young man by the name of Chris. They later married.

I resumed my previous life, enjoying the attractions of Bristol's social scene. I met up again with Marilyn, and we became regular cinemagoers. We developed a more platonic arrangement than previously, almost, but not quite, a brother and sister relationship. We were very comfortable with each other; just good friends.

A week or two after I split up with Lily I was again camping in the New Forest, this time just with Bernie. We were enjoying a cup of tea (it wasn't always beer) and noticed idly a couple of girls down the road who appeared to be hitch hiking. Unexpectedly, they left the road and walked up the track to our tent. What was extremely surprising was their identity, none other than Lily and her colleague from work, Judy. How come they were in the New Forest at the same time as us? Was she looking for me? If so, how did they discover our site? We were camping 'off-piste', not on a recognised site. I was stunned, but managed to speak to Lily,

'Amazing to see you, how are you? Can you stay?'

Lily said nothing, which did not surprise me, but Judy glanced at her, then turned to me,

'Ok, a cup of tea would be nice.'

I was dismayed with the sorry state of Lily, caused by my uncaring treatment of her.

Later, we took them to a club in Bournemouth and at the end of the evening dropped them off at their pre-booked B&B.

In spite of what Lily and I had been through, we kept in touch, enjoying dates from time to time, often with Lily spending the night in bed with me, just to sleep. We even spent two weeks camping in Cornwall the following September when we would originally have been on our honeymoon in the Scilly Isles. I admit that was bizarre. We remained on good terms throughout the holiday. I didn't tell anyone else about this arrangement as I would have felt awkward discussing it, but the truth came out later.

We camped at various delightful sites including Perranuthnoe, near Marazion and St. Michael's Mount. We visited the site of the Minack open air theatre at Porthcurno, a magical location for a romantic evening. We were close, both mentally and physically, that night. We did not move to a full entirety but shared intimate and special moments. We increased our knowledge of the female anatomy, which included surprises for us both.

I later contemplated how our future might have progressed had we stayed together and married. But I believe it would have been wrong to do so. Although difficult at the time to part, with emotions running high, we were both quite young and there was most certainly an issue with me not being sufficiently mature to settle down. I thought it right for us to go our separate ways.

20

JACKIE

An easy-going relationship
- most of the time

By the late 1960s I had served my time as a cashier and was transferred once again to the main city branch of the bank to further my training. It was here I met Jackie. I was a manager's assistant, she worked in the processing room. I don't know what it was that first attracted me to her, perhaps her endearing nature or her ready smile. She was also very affectionate company.

I was on good terms with my landlady at Roslyn Road. She asked if I would be so good as to collect the rent from the other tenants in the house on her behalf. She considered I must be a safe bet, being a bank clerk. I agreed, and in return asked if she would be prepared to pay the cost of installing Rediffusion in my flat. This was a very early form of cable TV. We agreed a deal and Jackie was the first to be entertained in this way.

Our dates consisted of the usual activities, spending quality time in my flat, and drinking at the many city and country pubs. Perhaps once in a while a meal out, which might be at a local omelette bar. Do we still have omelette bars? Or, for a special occasion, a steak in a Berni restaurant. Bristol was awash with Berni Inns. Invariably, a steak would be the main course, preceded by prawn cocktail and inevitably followed by black forest gateau. The high life indeed.

Some evenings might be a cinema visit. One such date of note was to see 'Romeo and Juliet' at ABC Whiteladies. I had parked the car across the road from the cinema - it was easier in those days. Driving away after the film, I hit an unmarked raised manhole cover, ripping a hole in the sump. I had no option but to pay for a taxi to take Jackie home as she lived some way from a bus route. This was the first time in my life I had paid for a taxi. It would be a while before I would experience a taxi ride myself, this not being the mode of transport used by impecunious youngsters.

I walked home, alone.

On another evening we were making our way to our preferred city cider house, the Coronation Tap, where I had previously worked during my Dursley days. Walking down the narrow cul-de-sac leading to the pub, I looked at her and thought she was looking good, especially striking. I spoke without thinking,

'You're looking smart tonight, Jackie.'

Wrong choice of words. She looked at me, not in a good way but with a frown. She had taken exception to the word *smart*, and was quite upset, more than I believed was really necessary. I meant she was looking attractive and should have said so. Our first tiff.

One weekend we were invited to a party in London which was to be held in a flat rented by Mac, who you may remember from the Mandrake night club incident a while ago. He worked in Fleet Street, in the days when the district was the centre of the printing and publishing industries. Mac asked if Jackie could bring a friend as currently, he did not have a girl. Jackie obliged and invited along a lively girl by the name of Viv. The three of us, together with a boot full of alcohol, drove up the A4 and eventually found his Finchley flat - without the aid of satellite navigation.

The party progressed well, albeit fairly innocently, but unfortunately Viv took a shine to one of Mac's colleagues. Understandably, this did not go down too well with Mac who later matched off to his bedroom, alone, slamming the door behind him, not to be seen again until the following morning. The rest of us bedded down on various sleeping bags and blankets in the only other room, in a top to toe arrangement. As I said, it was a fairly innocent party. We returned to Bristol.

Although I had now received a promotion, I was still short of cash. I placed an advert in the Evening Post for a male to share my flat with me. This is how I came to know the gentle and mild-mannered Jim. After a few months, however, he married his girlfriend Jane and moved out.

Once again, I was to be fully responsible for the albeit modest rent. I idly revealed this information to Jackie who came up with a possible solution, as she was considering leaving home.

'Why don't I move in?', she offered.

My initial reaction to this was - a great idea, bring it on! But just a minute, that sounds like it could become very close to a commitment. This thought alarmed me so I kind-heartedly, and a little sadly, turned down her generous offer. How different our lives might have been. Therefore no Jackie, but Richard moved in instead. In time he would take over the tenancy of the flat when I moved on.

Some while after my break with Lily, while I was dating Jackie, I heard about an Open Day at the Portishead nursery where Lily still worked. As Martin and Hazel were going to the event, I was encouraged to tag along. It seemed quite natural - at least to me - to take my current girlfriend Jackie with me on the outing. In the circumstances this was not the most tactful thing to do. I had not yet improved on my previous dubious record, still not a sensitive soul to the feelings of others.

Very soon, inevitably, Lily and Jackie met. Apparently one of Jackie's questions was,

'How many kids do you have here?'

When I next saw Lily on one of our casual dates, she told me how aghast she had been at Jackie's comment and reference to *kids*.

'That put me right off her, they are *orphaned children*', she exclaimed.

Hardly surprising, in the circumstances, that she did not hit it off with Jackie. My mistake, either I should not have attended the event, or most certainly should not have taken my latest flame with me.

At one point during the Open Day, Lily emerged from the nursery carrying a baby boy, and came across to me.

'Chris, this is my favourite, isn't he delightful? Would you like to hold him?'

We supported the baby between us, in our arms, looked at each other, and held our gaze for a moment longer than was perhaps appropriate. Memories stirred. I felt a tingling: an electrical charge was running through my body.

My apologies, I have digressed again; back to Jackie. There was one event when she embarrassed me, at a bank dinner dance. The evening started well, with drinks and socialising before taking our seats on the table reserved for our branch. There was no seating plan on the table as such and, as it turned out, Jackie ended up sitting next to the branch manager - my boss. I was horrified to watch Jackie eating her meal off her knife, I was sure everyone noticed. I was fearful as to how this behaviour would affect my career. These things mattered.

Jackie was a fan of Johnny Cash, as I was and still am today. One night we were watching the film 'At Folsom Prison' on the black and white TV in my flat. We were sitting on the floor, both engrossed in the film, with Jackie typically with her legs apart. This was her normal position, perhaps for comfort, when sitting casually. She was wearing a mini skirt, now around her waist. Quite revealing and perhaps not very ladylike, but I was enjoying the view. Her exposure might have been intentional - or not - but either way it was not my place to pass comment. In my naivety it didn't occur to me that her behaviour could have been an invitation, perhaps it was, perhaps not. If it was, where could that have led? A rhetorical question, I know full well where that could have led.

On a later evening, at my place, she said,

'You are not like all the other boys, all they want to do is get me into bed.'

I have mentioned more than once I was often too slow on the uptake. Hmm, is *that* an invitation? This time I must not lose the opportunity.

'Jackie, I would dearly love to go to bed with you, we could just lie down next to each other, under the covers.'

Worth a try, I thought.

'Yes alright, but we're not to do anything.'

I suggested she should take off her dress, simply to avoid getting it creased, mind. She agreed, removed her dress and tights, and we climbed into my single bed. I was up for it and I believed she was too, at least initially. I felt the start of her tantalising pubic hair as I edged the tips of my fingers up her inner thigh. She tensed. I edged closer as the stirring in my loins warned me to keep myself in control. I moved towards her, planning to use the withdrawal method. As soon as she felt me on the point of entering, she chickened out.

'I would do it with you, Chris, but no, I don't want to get pregnant.'

If only I had protection with me that night. We were both highly charged and passionate but hadn't taken any chances. Or had we?

On our next date, a few days later, an unusually quiet Jackie.

'You seem quiet, are you ok?' I questioned.

'It's alright.'

'Tell me, what's the matter?'

She was clearly very much on edge. I waited. After a moment she replied,

'I'm late.'

I froze and a cold sweat came over me. Déjà vu, I was reminded of the same scare I agonised over with Peggy. As it turned out, no pregnancy, relief all round. I told myself to stop taking these risks.

Sometime later, our relationship having drawn to a natural close, I knocked on the door of the flat where she now lived, in Zetland Road, purely to say 'Hello'. She took a while to answer, and I was about to walk away when she came to the door in a dishevelled state. Apparently, she shared the flat with Trevor, her latest boyfriend, and I had no doubt called at an embarrassing and inopportune moment. Was I the cause of unintended coitus interruptus? If they were enjoying themselves in the way I suspected, why did she bother to answer the door? Suffice to say I was not invited in, but she was very pleasant and I did win an affectionate peck on my cheek. I countered with a full mouth on mouth to which she responded in a most agreeable way.

21

IF MUSIC BE THE FOOD OF LOVE

It would be remiss to write about the 1960s without covering music - rock and pop in particular. It was a golden era for popular music, and still today some tracks remind me of certain girls:

'Things' by Bobby Darin - Janet;
'Happy Birthday Sweet Sixteen' by Neil Sedaka - Peggy;
'I'm into Something Good' by Herman's Hermits - Karen, at the start of our friendship, and
'You've Lost that Lovin' Feeling' by The Righteous Brothers, towards the end;
'I've Been Loving You Too Long' by Otis Redding - Marilyn;
'Days' by The Kinks - Lily;

'At Folsom Prison' by Johnny Cash - Jackie.
There were more.

'Some People' by Valerie Mountain reminds me of the film starring Kenneth More, of which the song was the title track; a film shot in Bristol including visions of the city, in particular the memorable motorcycle chase along the Portway. I loved it.

The musical press enjoyed a heyday during the 1960s with *Melody Maker, New Musical Express* (since renamed as *NME*) and others being popular publications. I bought my first copy of *New Musical Express* on my arrival in Bristol in January 1962. The headline read 'What's Twisting for 1962?' In the event, not as much as had been anticipated. Chubby Checker's two hits were released in 1960 and 1961 and his success was not repeated. 'The Twist' and 'Let's Twist Again' have been re-released several times since, and the dance has never disappeared from the scene completely.

In my early bedsit days, I decorated the room with a selection of lights and a road traffic lamp obtained with Bernard's help. This I converted to contain a red electric light bulb. In the environment created, I would set up my Dansette record player with a separate amplifier and extension speakers, kindly donated by Bernard. I was then ready to play my new and much improved collection of over 500 Sixties records.

This was well worthwhile preparation and created a warm atmosphere for entertaining. No wonder the landlord had a habit of complaining. Nowadays I am the one protesting about noise, in spite of being a little hard of hearing. Back then I couldn't understand why others didn't consider my music collection, and the volume at which it was played, as being just the greatest.

Bristol was alive with music across the city and is even more so today. We enjoyed concerts - at the Corn Exchange as I have already mentioned; the new Student Union in Upper Queen's Road; the Victoria Rooms - saw Pink Floyd there; and discos at various venues (the shortened version of discotheque had become prevalent by the later 1960s).

And there was, and still is, the Colston Hall, named after Edward Colston, a generous benefactor to Bristol. Colston's wealth was generated by the slave trade, though, and the Bristol Music Trust have decided that in 2020, after redevelopment, the hall will be renamed. A secondary reason for this name change might be the possibility of attracting a generous corporate sponsor.

At the time of writing there was a vociferous campaign against this decision, as many believe history can't be changed by changing a name and that by doing so, it is possible that in time the abhorrent slave trade would be forgotten. That must never happen.

As an aside, Bristol's prosperity was created not only from the slave trade, but also from tobacco and sherry. A puritanical city Bristol was not.

I enjoyed many shows at the Colston Hall. I failed to get seats for the Beatles, but did see the hysterical crowds outside the venue. I bought tickets to take Marilyn to see the late Otis Redding, a class act. I saw Cliff Richard with my sister. We sat on benches at the back of the stage and Cliff kindly turned round to acknowledge us from time to time. Others I saw at the hall included Helen Shapiro, Billy Fury, Eden Kane, Bobby Vee, Del Shannon, the Springfields, Billy J Kramer, Adam Faith, Ike and Tina Turner and many more. For some of these shows I would be joined by a group from my school days, who would travel up from Trowbridge.

The show to beat all shows, though, was the sensational Rolling Stones. Mike and I were very lucky to get tickets. Towards the end of the set by the support group (called bands nowadays, not groups) their lead guitar played Keith Richards' opening riff to 'Satisfaction'. The audience erupted into a frenzy of excitement which lasted until the Stones arrived on stage and continued throughout their entire performance; what a memorable evening.

22

GETTING THERE

Vanessa

A Unique Experience

One Saturday afternoon a quiet, dreamy girl, by the name of Vanessa looked in on me. I knew her vaguely from the Clyde Arms, the local Redland pub. I found myself in a highly unusual situation as she was looking for full sex, there and then. It took me a little while to realise this, but that indeed was her request.

I tried to fulfil her invitation but, due to a physical or an emotional issue, she was very constricted. I was not kitted out for the occasion but this was of no consequence as in the event little happened. She dressed and said she was leaving.

'I'll give you a lift home.'

'No thanks, it's ok.'
'It's no trouble, the car's outside.'
'No really, I'd prefer to walk.'

I reflect it is possible she was aware she had a problem and needed a young man to help her find a solution. Perhaps I should have persuaded her to stay and given her gentle encouragement, taking my time and, who knows, we might have reached a successful conclusion.

In spite of this being something of a non-event, a little later I noticed something unusual on my member, necessitating a visit to the Bristol Sexual Diseases Clinic. I was in luck, the tests proved negative.

Cynthia

Goodbye to what's left of innocence

I also met the voluptuous Cynthia at the local pub. Back to her place for coffee, made with dried milk which congealed on the surface. Quite dreadful. Her flat was not up to much either, and certainly not clean or tidy. She wasted no time in telling me,

'I'm going to slip into something more comfortable.'

Yes, she did actually use that phrase. She returned in a flimsy see-through negligee. Yes, I thought, that's comfortable - was she suggesting something? She certainly was. She took my hand and led me to her bedroom. She suggested I could undress and join her on her bed. I started to remove and neatly fold my clothes and place them on a chair. I have always been a fairly tidy person but in the circumstances, it is hard to believe I did that. She couldn't believe it either and cried out,

'Don't waste our time doing that, come over here!'

She was already lying naked on the bed. I joined her. Well, be rude not to. I closed my eyes so was not too sure what she was doing to my very firm erection, but it felt really nice. (I might be oversharing again.) She drew me into her. I backed out. Everything was happening far too quickly. Disappointed, she asked me,

'Why did you do that?'

I uttered the first words I could think of,

'Because I respect you too much.'

That might not have been strictly true.

(Note to self: don't get her pregnant.)

'Don't worry, I'm on the pill.'

Ah, well that's different. We agreed to meet again.

The following evening, we met in the same pub. One quick drink and off to her place. We both knew where the evening was heading and with the minimum of delay, gratefully no coffee this time, we were active on her bed. I moved to explore her body but she was not interested in any form of foreplay, preferring to move, without delay, to the main event. She was well versed in the activity. Previously, I had not progressed beyond a cautious and nervous entry followed by an almost immediate exit. How did I feel after this new episode in my life? A little dazed, perhaps, not quite an out of body experience (well, it was in one way). I felt strangely remote, as if in a dream. But a dream it was not. How was it for her? I didn't ask. She thanked me and we fell into a long and deep sleep. Well I did, and she agreed in the morning she had also slept well, and felt good. No lie in for me, though, as I had to return to my flat for a quick change into a suit, ready for work. We said our farewells.

I regret this experience was not sooner and, rather than being with Cynthia, had been with one of my genuine girlfriends, with a girl I cared for, with a girl I loved.

23

END OF AN ERA

Bristol has changed over the past 50 odd years, and not all to the good. Much of the city was destroyed during the Second World War and the city planners have been blamed for adding to this destruction. Clearly some criticism is justified, nevertheless the increasing volumes of traffic had to be managed somehow. Traffic was a problem back in the Sixties, but we didn't know we were born compared to the gridlocked roads of today.

Sadly, the shipbuilding and tobacco industries, amongst others, have disappeared, but the city has a thriving music and art scene and is well known for Wallace and Gromit, and Banksy; all is not lost.

And so to the end of the Sixties. 1969 was tinged with much sadness for me and my family as my brother Anthony, several years older and wiser than me, died from Hodgkin's Disease in Manchester Royal Infirmary on 11th November - Remembrance Day. In 1964 he met his true love at Manchester University, they married and settled in the city, later moving to Liverpool. Such a short life together; he will never be forgotten.

1970 was a turning point for many reasons, apart from having lost a very dear member of our family. Never again would such a decade be remembered for so much. I do remember those celebrated days, and remember them well.

The time from my arrival in Bristol in January 1962 until the dawn of the Seventies was filled with many special experiences. I count my blessings I was there, and fortunate in having made many good friendships, both male and female. I am still close to some of my male friends who shared the Sixties with me, but by the nature of things I am no longer in contact with my previous girlfriends. I have memories, though, from casual dates to long term relationships and everything in between. I was fond of them all and a few were very special, but, looking back throughout the Sixties, there was probably only one girl I truly loved.

I was lucky to have been born when I was and to have moved to Bristol when I did. My life could have been so different. I reflect that all the girls I met were white. Do I regret not having discovered intimacy with a girl from another ethnicity? The opportunities were limited, Bristol was not the cosmopolitan city it is today. My one experimental visit to a Caribbean club in St. Pauls was not successful in this respect.

Those I met, where are they all now? Are they still on this earth? And not just those I've mentioned, but all the other members of the youth clubs, the scooter club and the considerable number of work colleagues over the years. Where are they all?

The 1960s: I experienced my first love and beyond, and completed my journey from innocence. 1970 was the start of a new era for me. In June of that year I met a new girl and my life was about to change direction. But again to use a cliché, that is another story.

……………………...…………………

A note from the author

My grateful thanks for taking the time to read my narrative.

It would be much appreciated if you could spend a few moments writing a review for me on Amazon.

Thank you.

ABOUT THE AUTHOR

Chris Walker was born in Bristol in 1945, the day before VE Day. His mother once told him she was annoyed he arrived when he did. His birth led to her missing out on all the end-of-war celebrations in Bristol the next day as, being the 1940s, she was certainly not going to be allowed out of the nursing home so soon.

During the 1960s, he worked in various locations in and around Bristol and Avonmouth, developing an intimate knowledge of the city. Later, his employment necessitated moving to Farnham, Surrey where he now lives, but he is a regular visitor to Bristol. He has a vision of one day moving back to the city he has always loved.

If any reader should recognise themselves, in spite of some name changes, or if his reminiscing awakens recollections in others, Chris would be delighted if they were to get in touch to share memories of those glorious years.

ChrisWalker1812@gmail.com

Printed in Great Britain
by Amazon